The Style Guide

THE Style GUIDE

Sandra Wolton

Boxtree

First published in Great Britain in 1989
by Boxtree Limited
Published in association with
Independent Television Publications Ltd.

Designed by **Dave Goodman**
Illustrated by **Lynne Riding**
Front cover illustration by
Lynne Riding
Edited by **Charlotte Mortensson**
Typeset by **Action Typesetting Limited**,
Gloucester
Printed in Great Britain by
Richard Clay Limited, Bungay, Suffolk

For Boxtree Limited
36 Tavistock Street
London
WC2E 7PB

**British Library Cataloguing in
Publication Data**
Wolton, Sandra
  The style guide.
  1. Women's clothing. Fashion
  I. Title
  746.9′2

  ISBN 1–85283–273–8

Contents

Introduction

The idea of this book is to encourage you to take a fresh look at yourself and your STYLE. Whereas fashion is faddish, fickle, constantly changing, STYLE is of a different nature – it is altogether more calm, ongoing and lasting. STYLE is something which comes from within. It is not how much you spend – you can be stylish on a shoestring – it is how you project yourself, presenting a positive image which people will respond to favourably. STYLE is more than just carefully choosing your clothes, accessories, hair and make-up -- it is all of these things, plus every other aspect of your taste: your likes and dislikes, the interior of your home, in short, your whole environment.

It is not necessary to be young with model's proportions to look stylish. Most of us are less than perfect. It is far more important to work positively with your basic height, shape and colouring to create a style which you are happy with and which looks good.

Although I have offered lots of comments, hints, ideas and guidelines in this book, remember that there are no hard and fast rules. It is all down to you. Fashion and style should not be taken too seriously. Even though it is the face which one puts forward to the outside world it is not life or death!

The majority of people involved in

the fashion industry are notoriously scruffy or eccentric dressers, or both. Those in the business have the professional ability and confidence to transform themselves for the evening. They will present a total look which is a one-off, interpreted painstakingly by the individual for the occasion. For an opening, a party or any social event, there is an amazing metamorphosis. From the chrysalis emerges the most extraordinary butterfly! The next day, well, I am sure you can guess what happens. The scruff is back at his or her desk or studio. Creating STYLE? Maybe. Wearing it – not exactly. This approach shows a healthy irreverence towards fashion and STYLE.

The essence of STYLE is always confidence. A stylish person has a subtle self-awareness which comes from knowing that he or she looks good. Your clothes should become secondary, allowing you to project yourself one hundred per cent. Everyone has that potential.

On occasion, we have all put together 'looks' which have been disastrous. We have managed to get everything totally wrong, all in one go! At a time like this, confidence can go a long way towards salvaging the situation. It is possible to come out of it smiling, with those around you still thinking of you as a woman with lots of STYLE.

Sandra Wolton

CHAPTER ONE

Bodycare Basics

★ Warming up ★

★ Selecting your exercise ★

★ You are what you eat! ★

★ Skincare ★

★ Bathtime ★

★ Focussing on hands and feet ★

★ Your hair ★

★ Stress – a modern malaise ★

Your outer appearance relies enormously upon the regular maintenance of your body. Exercise is important in order to remain fit and healthy, as is diet. Whatever your size or shape, it is possible to tone your body. You will feel healthier and your clothes will look much better on you. Stylish clothes will not hide a flabby body or avert attention from messy hair and unhealthy-looking skin, so in order to look good, you must look after yourself. This is true for all ages and is equally essential for both women and men. Health is the single most important concern for every individual, and children should be taught the rudiments of bodycare and encouraged to carry on these important routines throughout their lives.

You must, however beware. Exercise, fitness and diet are a very big business for a growing number of people. Every spring, as sure as we see crocuses and daffodils popping their delicate heads through the earth, we are confronted by a fresh crop of exercise routines, diets and sundry ideas, all encouraging us to improve our bodies – and spend money. All you can do is skim through the sales talk and use your common sense.

This section offers you ideas and tips; then, basically, it is down to you!

Warming up

If your car is only used in town, stopping and starting and rarely getting into fourth gear, the engine gradually gets more and more clogged up, thus reducing efficiency. What it needs is a good blast on a longer journey, so that the whole system can get back into working order. Similarly, many of us sit behind a desk from Monday to Friday, travel to and from work by train or bus and jump into the car to get to the shops at the weekend. In short, we never get out of second gear! This way of life leaves our bodies in dire need of exercise. Our limbs need to be stretched, used, exerted, to be kept in good working order. The heart and lungs need to be subjected to periods of strenuous exercise in order to remain healthy.

It is important to be realistic when planning a fitness regime for yourself. It will be a lot easier to achieve a certain degree of success if you decide what your motives are. Perhaps you have simply gained weight; you may feel that your body could benefit by being toned. You may be aware that you have let things slide and that you now have less stamina than you used to. Once you have established what you want to achieve and why, assess your lifestyle and your habits. Begin by making a few changes to your way of life, but do not be too ambitious or too impatient.

You can re-introduce exercise into your life by walking rather than using the car or taking public transport. It is one of the best forms of exercise available and does not cost a penny. You will soon start to feel much healthier if you get into the habit of taking brisk walks several times a week.

Fun for all the family

Walking, running, cycling, swimming, tennis and lots of other activities can be enjoyed by all members of the family. If you have a favourite sports activity introduce it to your children early on – your enthusiasm will probably rub off on them. Make a point of regularly taking them to the park. WALK to the park. Have a RUN around with the kids when you get there. Go for a run alongside them while they CYCLE. Take a ball with you – have a family game of FOOTBALL. Go for a SWIM with your kids. You will enjoy it enormously. If they are small, make sure that you have another adult with you so that you can do a few lengths on your own. You need exercise just as much as your children do.

B
O
D
Y
C
A
R
E

B
A
S
I
C
S

BODY LINES

Selecting your exercise

Whatever your age, exercise improves your physical fitness, helps you to relax, relieves stress and works off tension, tiredness and lethargy. It also keeps your joints oiled, your heart and lungs healthy and your spine strong and mobile.

The benefits of exercise are undeniable, but how do you know which will be the most effective for you? Fitness, like clothes, goes through various styles and vogues. 'Experts' are continuously coming up with new theories which will, supposedly, answer all our problems.

The word 'aerobic' is coined daily in connection with exercise. Remember Jane Fonda going for the 'big burn' several years ago? Since then, the pendulum has swung towards 'low impact' aerobics which is not so strenuous. 'Aerobic' simply means that an exercise puts the body under steady stress, thereby increasing the heart rate and pumping more blood around the body. Aerobic exercise builds up stamina, strength and endurance. Although we associate the word with dance-style work-outs, swimming, skipping, running, jogging, cycling, walking and rowing are all aerobic exercises.

ON THE RIGHT TRACK

The essentials for running are a tracksuit and good quality running shoes. For longer distances – shed the tracksuit and wear a singlet and shorts.

The basic requirements of aerobic exercise are:

★ You must maintain the activity for 20 to 30 minutes. If you have not exercised for a while, start with shorter sessions of 5 to 10 minutes and gradually build up the time.

★ The exercise must be intense enough to raise your pulse to between 110 to 160 beats per minute.

★ To avoid straining your muscles, warm up and stretch before you begin the exercise.

The exercise chart below gives basic information about the benefits of the sports and activities which are available to most people. When choosing one for yourself remember that the way to begin exercising is little by little, and often. Choose an exercise which will comfortably fit into your schedule and, most important of all, choose something which really appeals to you. The essential thing is to enjoy it and to continue to do so!

A quick run down

BADMINTON
Keeps the body supple and helps develop co-ordination and quick reflexes. Suitable for all age groups and very easy and quick to learn.

CYCLING
Excellent aerobic exercise for the heart and lungs. Develops the leg muscles very quickly. People with weak backs should ensure that the handlebars are not too low in relation to the saddle. Suitable for all age groups but children must take a cycling course before going on the road.

EXERCISE/DANCE CLASSES
Will improve suppleness, strength and co-ordination. Whatever type of class you choose – ballet, tap, jazz, stretch – make sure that your teacher is fully qualified.

JOGGING
Good aerobic exercise for the heart and lungs. Develops muscle tone in the legs. To avoid damage to knee or hip joints, jog on soft ground and wear a good-quality pair of running shoes. Suitable for all age groups, but build up jogging time gradually, starting with just five minutes.

RIDING
Tones legs and bottom and develops balance and co-ordination. Not suitable for people with back or knee problems. Can be enjoyed by all age groups.

SQUASH
Improves stamina and agility and develops hand to eye co-ordination. Squash is very strenuous and is best enjoyed by people who take regular vigorous exercise.

SWIMMING
Good for overall fitness, this sport increases stamina and strength and maintains suppleness. Backstroke is particularly good for people with back problems as it strengthens the muscles around the spine. Suitable for all age groups as there is little danger of over-straining muscles.

TABLE TENNIS
Improves agility and co-ordination and helps to develop faster reflexes. Suitable for all age groups and all levels of fitness – it can be as fast or as leisurely as you like.

TENNIS
Works on the whole body, strengthening the heart, lungs, legs, stomach, back and shoulders. People who play a lot of tennis will find that their racquet arm and shoulder develops more than the other side. Tennis is a strenuous sport and participants should be fit and used to regular, vigorous exercise.

WALKING
Gently tones the whole body. Aim for a brisk pace which keeps you puffing and will exercise your heart and lungs.

You are what you eat!

Never before have we been so aware of the benefits of a balanced diet. Apart from improving the condition of your skin and hair, eating sensibly will often stabilise your weight. A balanced diet consists of plenty of fresh fruit and vegetables and lots of fibre, which is found in wholegrain cereals, brown rice, wholewheat pasta and wholemeal bread. It is a good idea to cut down the amount of caffeine you consume and to eat fish and white meat, rather than red meat.

Make sure that you drink at least a

litre of water a day and try starting each morning with a glass of fresh fruit juice. Drinking plenty of fluids will keep your skin fresh and clear.

Fats and oils can have an adverse effect on our blood cholesterol levels. Our bodies naturally produce adequate amounts of this fatty substance and it is not necessary to take in extra amounts. As we get older, deposits can build up in our arteries, leading to serious health problems. A high cholesterol level in our blood will speed up this process. It is, therefore, important to cut down on the amount of fats and oils that we consume. When you are selecting a cooking oil try to buy safflower, sunflower, corn or soya bean oil.

Watch your weight

There are certain guidelines which we should not ignore. While it is not desirable to become obsessive about diet and weight, being drastically over- or under-weight will cause health problems. If you are wildly out of line and carrying far too much weight, you are usually aware of it. Everyone knows in their heart of hearts when they are sticking to a balanced diet and when they are eating to excess. Unless you are ill, there is not much excuse for being drastically overweight. Try to maintain a size at which you feel reasonably fit. Remember, whatever your size, do not overeat. Even if you are really slim, overeating can cause coronary heart disease which is responsible for four out of ten deaths in this country.

Over-indulgence in food, alcohol or cigarettes will create toxins (organic poisons) which your body then has to get rid of. Imagine your liver as a vast recycling plant which converts toxins into substances which can be easily eliminated. Your liver has the task of detoxifying alcohol, while your kidneys filter your blood. Overloading our bodies with unnecessary food and poisons will quickly lead to unpleasant side effects including a general susceptibility to infections, over-production of mucus, oily hair and skin, spots, bad breath, body odour and a general loss of energy and vitality. Obviously toxins are to be avoided!

A quick remedy

Eliminate toxins from your body with this four-day fruit and vegetable fast. It is safe and easy and will give your overworked liver and kidneys a well-earned break.

Day One: Eat only fresh fruit and raw or lightly cooked vegetables. Drink only pure unsweetened fruit juice, diluted with bottled spring water and a twist of lemon.

Days Two and Three: Eat only non-citrus fruits, particularly grapes, apples, pears, bananas, kiwi fruit and melons. Drink the same as specified for Day One.

Day Four: Repeat Day One.

Moderate exercise will speed up the detoxification process, so go for a gentle walk each day. Drink at least a pint of water each day of the fast, to avoid dehydration. Thereafter, introduce herbal teas and plenty of freshly-squeezed fruit and vegetable juices. Avoid coffee, tea and alcohol for at least one week after the four-day period.
NOTE: Some people may experience side effects such as slight headaches, nausea or temporarily worsening skin conditions. However, by Day Three you will feel fitter and mentally clearer, so it is well worth persevering.

Stop smoking

Cigarettes are lethal. They will also spoil your looks. Smoking slows the circulation near the skin's surface, giving it a sallow tone. The action of drawing on a cigarette deepens wrinkles around the mouth.

Skincare

Good skin is an integral part of a stylish appearance. From adolescence onwards, it is essential to spend a little time first thing in the morning and last thing at night, looking after your skin. The basic skincare steps are very straightforward – CLEANSE, TONE, NOURISH. These simple routines will ensure that most skins are kept reasonably clean and healthy although, of course, the menstrual cycle will affect your complexion. However, regular maintenance will help enormously!

When cleansing, the cream or lotion should be applied to the cheeks, nose,

Facing the elements

Protect your skin during cold weather with an extra rich moisturiser. Try using Vaseline as a night cream to feed your skin.

★

Always protect your face and your body with a good sun screen. Wear sunglasses to avoid damage to the eyes themselves and wrinkling of the skin around the eyes.

---

forehead, chin and neck and gently massaged with your finger tips using small circular movements. The area around the eyes should be wiped very gently. Remove the cream with cotton wool and repeat the process until the cotton wool looks clean. Dab the toner onto the skin using cotton wool. This will close the pores and freshen the skin. For the final stage, put a little moisturiser onto your finger tips and apply the cream or lotion with gentle, massaging strokes.

Many readers will already have their favourite skincare products. There are, however, certain guidelines which will assist you in caring for your particular type of skin.

Normal/Combination skin
Daytime: Use a light cleansing milk or facial wash, followed by skin freshener. Finish with a light moisturising lotion on the dry areas.
Nighttime: Apply a slightly richer moisturiser.
Extras: Use a gentle, non-drying exfoliator once or twice a week. Apply a stimulating face mask once a week.

Oily skin
Daytime: Use an oil-free cleanser or cleansing soap to dissolve excess oils. Apply a mild astringent. Use a non-greasy moisturiser to protect your skin from the elements.
Nighttime: Use an anti-bacterial face wash on any spot-prone area. Apply a light, oil-free moisturiser on dry areas.
Extras: Use a deep cleansing exfoliator on problem areas twice a week. Apply a medicated face pack once a week to brighten the skin and draw out impurities.

Dry skin
Daytime: Do not use soap. Wash with a creamy cleanser to leave the skin feeling moist. Apply a mild toning rinse and moisturise with a rich lotion.
Nighttime: Use a rich night cream as well as an eye cream.
Extras: Use concentrated creams or lotions for extra moisturising. Use a moisturising face mask once a month. Avoid strongly perfumed products.

Dry/Sensitive skin
Daytime: Use hypo-allergic skin products and avoid soap and perfumed products. Always use an alcohol-free skin freshener and a moisturiser to protect your skin against the cold. If you have broken veins, use a cream which aids repair.
Nighttime: For extra gentle cleansing use luke-warm water and apply a night cream formulated for sensitive skins.
Extras: Do not use exfoliating creams or lotions on skin which is prone to broken veins.

Never use perfumed products – even deodorants should be perfume-free.

★

Wear soft, natural fabrics next to the skin. Avoid wearing wool or anything rough.

★

Avoid long soaks in the bath. They will dry out your skin and increase irritation.

★

Only wear 18 carat gold, British sterling silver, stainless steel or platinum earrings.

★

Avoid foods which contain additives or preservatives. They often cause or aggravate allergies.

Bathtime

Whether you are six or 60, bathtime can be full of delights. Use the time to treat yourself to an easy, home-beauty routine which is guaranteed to rejuvenate and relax you.

First of all, take the telephone off the hook, turn the lights down low and the music up. Gather together the things that you will need – a gentle face mask, a loofah and a pumice stone. Add your favourite oil or foam to the bath, and we will begin.

Step One: Remove all traces of make-up with a creamy cleanser and apply the face mask, which should be left on for 10 to 15 minutes.

Step Two: Using the loofah, give yourself a vigorous scrub all over to get rid of all the surface grime and dead cells and stimulate your circulation.

Step Three: Now that you have soaked for a while, your skin will have softened. Gently scrub the soles of your feet, your elbows and any other areas of dry skin with a pumice stone.

Step Four: Dry yourself with a friction towel. You will feel fresh, invigorated and ready to face the world again!

BODYCARE BASICS

Focussing on hands and feet

Well-manicured hands and feet play an important part in creating an overall image. Obviously, your feet are not in view as often as your hands, but they should be well-looked after in the summer, at least. Nails should be massaged once a week with warm almond oil which feeds and strengthens them. The cuticles can be gently eased back with an orange stick or your fingers.

On your hands, the nails should be neatened using an emery board. Always file towards the centre. If your nails tend to be brittle, massage Vaseline or a hand cream around the base of your nails every day. Your choice of polish should be made according to the condition of your hands and nails. If you do not want to draw attention to them, use a base coat and a neutral colour. However, if they are in excellent condition, you can use as vibrant a colour as you please!

The nails on your feet should be clipped straight across. This discourages ingrowing toenails. Smooth the nails with an emery board. Use small wedges of cotton or tissue to keep the toes apart when applying polish.

Your hair

Your hair needs to work as part of your total look. Along with your clothes, it is an integral part of your image. Like all areas of style, your choice of cut follows a pattern of experimentation through the teens and twenties and tends to settle in your thirties, after which it changes very little. It is important to keep an open mind about your hair, whatever your age. Have a look at hairstyles in magazines and on the street. Reassess your hairstyle every now and then. Ask a good friend for their *honest* opinion about your present style.

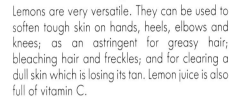

Natural beauty

Live yoghurt can be used as an effective face mask for combination skins. Spread it over the face and neck, avoiding the eyes and mouth. Leave it on for ten minutes, then tissue the mask off. Splash your face with tepid water to remove any residue. Yoghurt will also take the sting out of dry or sensitive skin.

★

Lemons are very versatile. They can be used to soften tough skin on hands, heels, elbows and knees; as an astringent for greasy hair; bleaching hair and freckles; and for clearing a dull skin which is losing its tan. Lemon juice is also full of vitamin C.

★

Drink eight glasses of water a day to flush toxins from your body.

Choosing a style

It is essential to maintain an overall sense of scale and proportion when assessing your hairstyle. You must create a balanced image. If you are a big lady, extremely short or very long hair will not flatter your shape – unless you are a wild extrovert! I know one such lady who crops her hair savagely and looks great, but she is one of the exceptions. Usually, extreme lengths will exaggerate size. If you are naturally gamine, short boyish cuts will suit you. Chic, one-length bobs will look great on people of average or tallish height with a fairly slender build. Short people should avoid cuts which are shoulder length or longer because they 'cut' the image, unless you are very well proportioned. Instead, look for a shorter style which is in scale with you as a whole and allows some of your neck and shoulders to be visible.

You should also give some thought to the type of image you want to portray: Hard and stylised? Soft and feminine? High fashion? Your hair must relate to the 'looks' you are creating with your clothes.

You should aim for versatility and ease with your hair. Consider its texture and choose a style which is appropriate. Constantly straightening natural ringlets is a waste of time, as is trying to coax curls into hair which is destined to be poker straight. You want your hair to look good all the time, so you require a cut which you can cope with yourself – unless you have the time and the money to make weekly visits to your hairdresser.

There are certain basic styles which are always in fashion, with slight re-interpretations every now and again. The list below will enable you to assess which of these may be suitable for you and your lifestyle.

Geometric Cuts: Most suitable for straight hair, but will work with curly hair if it is quite short. There are a lot of variations to this theme, but geometric cuts usually look best on the very young.

The Bob: This style is usually seen on straight hair, but can look just as good with curls. It emphasises the shine and texture of the hair and is easy to vary with hair accessories. The bob usually looks best on people in their teens and twenties with light, swingy hair. The severity of the style can be softened with a fringe.

Shaggy Hair: Ideal for curly or permed hair, although it can work with straight hair. This cut looks wonderful with highlights and lowlights. The style can be translated into a variety of shapes, according to how it is graded, but it still needs regular trimming, or you end up looking like an Old English Sheepdog!

The Crop: Works with most types of hair. It can look fabulous, but needs frequent trimming and a certain amount of confidence! The severity of the cut can be toned down by using gels or mousses. The style looks very effective with strong colours.

Hair care

Hair soon becomes dull and lank because of the dust and debris in the atmosphere. Most people have to wash their hair at least twice a week. Use a shampoo which is appropriate to your type of hair, avoiding harsh products which will overdry it.

As with skin, hair needs lots of tender loving care. It takes a lot of punishment from the elements and any chemical treatments we may use. It is, therefore, essential to condition your hair after every wash. For a more lasting conditioning system, try colourless henna wax.

When drying your hair, do not use the drier at full, hot blast. Warm air will dry it just as quickly and with less damage. If your hair is straight and fine, dry the roots with your head held upside down. This will give it more volume and bounce.

Hints on hair

If your hair begins to look dry and lifeless even when it is freshly washed, you may need to remove a build up of gel, spray or mousse. Use a shampoo which is specially formulated for this purpose to give it back its lustre.

★

Give your brushes and combs a weekly scrub. Rinse them thoroughly and allow moisture to drain from the base.

★

Never use elastic bands on your hair – they cause a lot of damage. Use fabric covered bands instead.

★

To distribute mousse or gel evenly on the hair, put it on your palms first and then apply it to your damp hair. Remember, a little goes a long way.

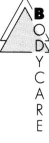

Opposite

1 Balance a **longer** face with a cut which frames this shape more softly. Long straight sides will not flatter.

2 An **oval** face looks great with geometric lines and fuller sides.

3 A crop with a longer crown and some softness complements a **round** face.

4 Flatter a **square** shape with a more dramatic chin-length bob.

Stress – a modern malaise

The pace of our lives has certainly become much faster in recent years. Our expectations – of ourselves and our lifestyles – have risen, so we try to cram more and more into our already busy days in order to achieve our aspirations. There are constant pressures put on us by advertising and the media to conform to today's ideals. Young people, in particular, are electing to take on responsibilities earlier and earlier. Lots of young singles are buying their own flats or houses, and acquiring financial burdens much sooner than their parents chose to.

On a more positive note, many experts feel that stress comes from within the individual and is a natural bodily reaction which enables us to tackle emergencies and problems to our best ability. It is only when we constantly go into overdrive, tensing and approaching every problem, however small, with adrenalin pumping, that we start to suffer seriously from 'stress'. We have to learn to recognise when this likely to happen and to avoid responding in this way. It does not solve any problem more successfully, and it leaves us feeling drained, 'wound up' and even more exhausted. This approach, over a period of time, can become a threat to health.

Unfortunately, stressful feelings can become such an everyday occurance, that you cease to be aware of them, until something snaps. It is important, therefore, to monitor your feelings and your reactions to people and events, and to give yourself a break – even if it is just a walk around the block – when you think that things are reaching boiling point.

One thing is for certain – stress and style do not go hand in hand. Constant feelings of tension are clearly reflected in the face: the mouth becomes set and hard and the eyes vague and unfocussed. Anxious, pressurised people look troubled and unapproachable – and much older than they need to. Tension also becomes trapped in the body. Joints and muscles stiffen; shoulders ache and the upper and lower areas of the back hurt. Posture is usually affected, leading to a stiff gait, with shoulders aggressively thrust back, or round shoulders and a shuffling walk. We may not even be aware of our facial expressions or bad postural habits – they creep up on us over the years – but they will certainly not enhance any outfit. A calm, untroubled face and a confident, springy walk are our most important fashion accessories.

So how do we prevent life's burdens from wearing us down? There is a lot we can do.

Spoil yourself

However little spare time or cash you may have, aim to treat yourself every now and then to a massage, a sauna or a steam treatment. Massage, in particular, is a wonderful way of relieving symptoms of stress. There are many different types of massage, from 'Swedish', which involves a lot of 'slapping' and 'cupping' and can even be rather painful, to gentler methods. Ask the salon precisely what is involved and make sure that the masseusse is fully qualified and experienced – it is important that she knows her job thoroughly in order for it to be a relaxing experience for you. Alternatively, perhaps you could invest in a book about massage and persuade your partner to do it instead?

Aromatherapy is a popular form of massage, during which essential oils are used. The oils are thought to draw out impurities from the body and to induce a feeling of deep relaxation. Minor ailments such as sinus trouble or aches and pains are also said to be alleviated by aromatherapy.

Saunas and steam baths are certainly very relaxing, as well as being good for the skin. Try one or the other after a strenuous swim – you will feel physically invigorated, and much calmer mentally.

Exercise

Regular exercise, whether it is a structured class or just a daily walk, will contribute a great deal towards alleviating stress, and will ensure that your body does not store up symptoms of stress in the muscles and joints. Try to incorporate a few stretching exercises into your daily routine. Many people find that very hard, exhausting sports, such as squash or a long run, get rid of all the aggression that has built up in them during the day. It is certainly a preferable alternative to venting your anger and frustration on your family or work colleagues!

A change of scenery is an important way of alleviating stress. At the end of an office day, you may leave feeling exhausted but, after a brisk walk and a few breaths of fresh air, you will start to revive. After a day at home looking after young children, you may feel tired, but getting out, even if it is only for a short while, to an exercise class or for a swim, will do you the world of good. The change will give you a different focus on life, and you will feel ten times better.

Here are some hints for creating a less stressful day.

At home

★ Vary the pace of your day. It is all too easy to work hard right through the day and completely exhaust yourself.

★ Give yourself a break in the day. Go out at lunchtime, or meet a friend for coffee in the morning.

★ Try to avoid peak hours in shops – crowded supermarkets really are very stressful and very hard work.

★ Try to plan the structure of your day – it will avoid panics later on. Set aside a little time in each day, which is to be spent on you. Even if it is just half an hour, do something which is just for you.

★ Have a night off each week. Go out with your partner, friends, or on your own, if you prefer. Try a new sport or a new exercise class. Alternatively, stay in with a good book, or spend the evening in the bath!

At work

★ Allow plenty of time to prepare for meetings and appointments.

★ If you can, take the pressure off, by delegating responsibility to juniors.

★ If you do have difficult work relationships, keep calm. Never anticipate rows or problems – they often don't materialise!

★ Try to vary the routine of your working day as much as possible. Go out and do something at lunchtimes.

★ If your job is sedentary, make a point of incorporating some exercise into your day. Have a swim before you go to the office, or fit in an exercise class at the end of the day.

Don't rely on props

However much pressure we are under, it is imperative that we avoid turning to drink, alcohol or tranquilisers. Unfortunately, our society often sees these drugs as an acceptable way of coping with stress, but they can only harm us in the long run, and will make problems more difficult to tackle.

CHAPTER TWO

Body Shape

★ The female form ★

★ Figure types ★

★ Shape and fashion ★

★ Sizing ★

★ Shape and history ★

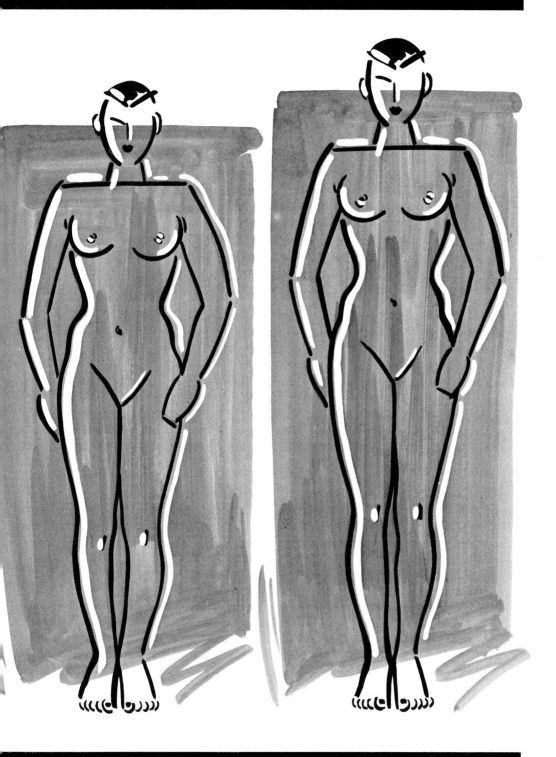

Before buying new clothes, you must consider your shape. Your height and body proportions are the factors which will, largely, determine which styles will look good on you.

The female form

Before you become at all disheartened about your figure, I would like to point out that, despite female 'liberation', 'feminism' and 'post feminism', the way in which women are portrayed in the media and in advertising is still unrealistically thin. The female body is a wonderful, unique shape, worthy of celebration. It is naturally curvy. A reclining woman is one glorious undulation of bust, waist, hips and legs. Our shape is our shape, and we should be proud of it. As long as you are healthy, you must learn to think of yourself and your body shape positively. ACCEPT IT AND ENJOY IT!

Familiarise yourself with the types of clothes that you like, the lines and the ideas which are flattering – and then have the confidence to wear them. In this section, I have offered options, suggestions and guidelines to help you recognise which styles you are likely to look good in. At all costs, do not regard the advice as rules and regulations. Ultimately, it is up to you to translate the information into practical terms.

Figure types

The following information is a breakdown of the main categories of shapes. Decide which one is the most accurate description of your build and use the information to assist you in buying clothes which suit you.

Short with a slender frame

A simple approach to style which many petite ladies adopt, is to emphasise your femininity. Wearing well proportioned classically tailored separates and suits will achieve this effect. Softer, more fluid and feminine blouses, skirts and dresses can also look very good. Make sure that the style is not too nipped in and neat. It will only over-emphasise small stature, resulting in you looking even tinier. You must develop a keen eye for scale and proportion when choosing clothes.

Hip or three-quarter length jackets, very short or very long skirts and trousers with turn-ups should all be avoided. Exaggerated, dramatic shapes with bolder detail have not been designed with your dimensions in mind and they will swamp a petite frame.

If you are flat chested and tend to be bony, do not wear V-necks or plunging necklines which will emphasise thinness. Choose looser, softer necklines and try wearing horizontal stripes, small shoulder pads or layered looks to give an impression of width.

Short with an average frame

The same principles as above apply to you but, as you are a bit 'meatier' you can afford to bend the rules slightly. Clingy, tight clothes can look great on a well proportioned, petite lady. Avoid fussy clothes or anything with too much detail.

Short and rounded

Simplicity is the key. You want to create an illusion of length by focussing on your good points and diverting attention away from the extra weight. Avoid horizontal stripes, checks or patterns which define your shape too drastically. If you have a large bust, large waist or large hips, select styles which are not too tight over the problem area. Choose the cut of your clothes carefully so that they do not stop at your widest part. For instance, if your waist is large, choose hip-length jackets and tops. Large hips can be disguised with floppy trousers, loose tunics and drop waisted dresses.

If you do not have one 'problem area', but are large all over, you may as well have some fun with your clothes. You are large – so what! A friend of mine who is a short, rounded lady breaks every rule in the book and looks wonderful ALL the time. Her main attributes are a shock of red curly hair and a wonderful sense of colour which she uses to full advantage. On this lady, it is an extremely successful approach!

Large ladies

If you have problems finding clothes which you like, try the specialist shops and ranges. They have improved tremendously over the last couple of years and usually stock fashionable, interesting styles.

★

Avoid flirty or childish styles. 'Peter Pan' collars, bunchy skirts and pretty ribbons are definitely not a good idea.

★

If you are a large lady with a confident disposition, why not throw care to the wind and dress as you please! Make the most of your size – large people can look fabulous!

★

Lots of larger ladies are snapping up men's garments. Shirts, sweaters, classic macs and trench coats are often made in the most fabulous fabrics and can look extremely chic.

★

If you can spare the time, dressmaking can produce fabulous results. The trick is to find a good pattern and then adapt it so that it fits you perfectly.

General notes for short people

It IS possible to give the illusion of additional height by clever dressing. One of the easiest ways is to direct attention from the waist. Try wearing thin belts on the hip rather than the waist to elongate the torso. Wear long necklaces and scarves, and use shoulder bags with long straps. All of these touches will take the emphasis away from the waist. Smaller, narrower lapels will also add to the illusion of extra height.

Resist the temptation of adding extra inches with very high heels. They destroy the proportion and balance of any outfit, and they look ghastly! You will simply look like a small person desperately trying to look taller!

Exaggerated textures such as mohair, bouclé and thick, long-haired fur should also be avoided – being a small creature, you will be in dire danger of disappearing completely from view! The same advice applies to large, flamboyant prints and over-sized accessories. Too much clutter of any kind – fancy buttons, epaulettes, fussy jewellery – should be avoided.

Medium height with a slight frame

Many of the guidelines given to the short petite person will apply to you. However, you are more fortunate in that there is a wider selection of clothes for you in the shops because you are approaching the 'standard' size. Softer, swathed and draped lines will flatter your build. There is a danger of being swamped, so keep away from huge jackets, tops, dresses and coats – they will over-emphasise your slenderness. If you are very slim, avoid tight clothes. When you dress for drama, remember that a little goes a long way. In terms of accessories and extra-complicated touches, it is not down to how much you wear – it is the boldness with which you wear it that counts.

Medium height with an average frame

Finding clothes is not a problem for you. You can successfully carry off more flamboyant and extreme styles, should you want to. You will find that most fashion stores will suit your build. Being a 'standard' size, you have more leeway to be adventurous.

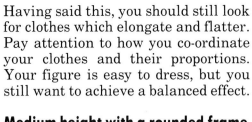

Having said this, you should still look for clothes which elongate and flatter. Pay attention to how you co-ordinate your clothes and their proportions. Your figure is easy to dress, but you still want to achieve a balanced effect.

Medium height with a rounded frame

You want to flatter your good points and draw attention from any flaws. This can be done by choosing shapes carefully. If you are especially big busted, big waisted or big hipped, select styles which are loose over those areas and avoid prints which emphasise them. If you are large all over, try shirts, sweaters, sweatshirts or dresses which are a longer, tunic shape. Trousers should have simple waists and be particularly loose on the thighs. Skirts can be more difficult. Keep to simple designs and avoid pleating or gathering on the waist. Do not choose very short skirts or vivid colours. Dresses will make most impact if the style is loose and fairly feminine. Fabrics should not be too textured.

Tall with a slight frame

The world is your oyster because you are the ideal 'clothes horse'. Yours is the figure which the world's top designers choose for showing and selling their wares. You can afford to be more dramatic and wear bolder clothes. You must, however, still consider the scale, proportion and balance of your outfits carefully. Less defined shapes can make a tall woman look gawky and ungainly. Never wear 'little girlish' dresses.

You will look good in body skimming clothes, tight pants and skirts of any length. It is often more attractive to create a womanly shape with your clothes but, if you prefer, you can focus on your slimness. Avoid vertical stripes and rectangular shapes which will over-emphasise your slim build; it is great to be tall and skinny, but don't overdo it!

Opposite
Whatever your shape, it is important to be aware of the areas to emphasise, and of those parts which sometimes could do with a spot of camouflage. The main aim is to focus on your good points and, through the way you dress, to divert attention from any problem areas, creating as much of a sense of balance as possible. Although these three figures are all of average build, they should consider their differences in height when choosing clothes to create a well-proportioned image.

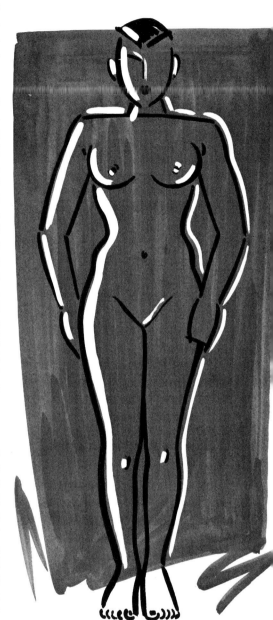

You HAVE to present yourself with a lot of confidence. Tall people always make a dramatic entrance, whether they want to or not! They cannot blend into the background, so learn how to carry your height proudly.

Tall with a medium frame
Your height will give an illusion of slimness, so you can choose styles

B
O
D
Y

S
H
A
P
E

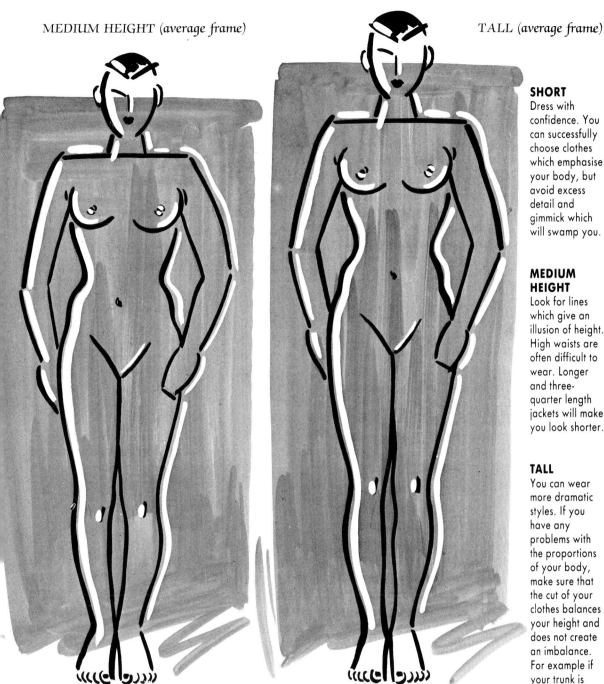

MEDIUM HEIGHT (average frame)

TALL (average frame)

SHORT
Dress with confidence. You can successfully choose clothes which emphasise your body, but avoid excess detail and gimmick which will swamp you.

MEDIUM HEIGHT
Look for lines which give an illusion of height. High waists are often difficult to wear. Longer and three-quarter length jackets will make you look shorter.

TALL
You can wear more dramatic styles. If you have any problems with the proportions of your body, make sure that the cut of your clothes balances your height and does not create an imbalance. For example if your trunk is longer you can successfully wear high waist trousers and skirts, and if you have longer legs you will look good in hip-length tops.

which emphasise any aspect of your figure that you wish. You will look good in most styles. Avoid clothes with horizontal stripes or large shoulder pads and steer clear of very heavy textures — you don't want to look enormous!

Tall and rounded

If extra weight is concentrated in mainly one area such as your hips, waist or bust, make sure that your clothes fit loosely over the trouble spot. The fact that you are tall will divert attention from any extra padding. If you are big all over, do not wear tight clothes — it never works! Keep your styles simple and dramatic, if you want to, and avoid prints which closely follow your shape.

27

This group of figures are all of average height, but their body frames differ considerably. When dressing they must take their shape into consideration to create an harmonious and well-balanced image. Read our hints opposite to help them out.

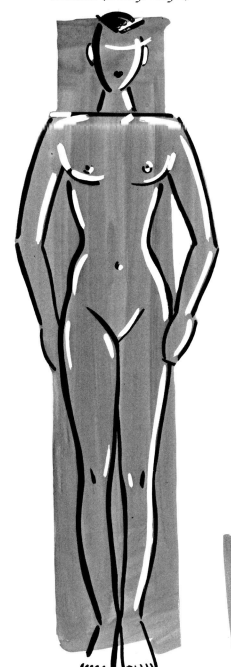

SLIGHT (average height)

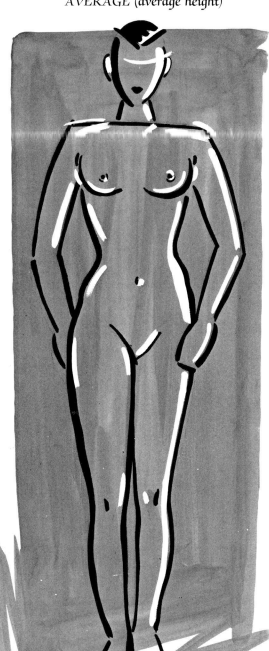

AVERAGE (average height)

Disguise and flatter

As a general rule when choosing clothes, you can afford to skim and flatter your good points and should go for a looser fit where a spot of camouflage is required.

Clothes to enhance your silhouette

Blouses
★ Wide cuffs will make your arms look shorter.
★ Slimmer sleeves balance a large bust.
★ Floppy or fuller sleeves are kinder to chubby arms.

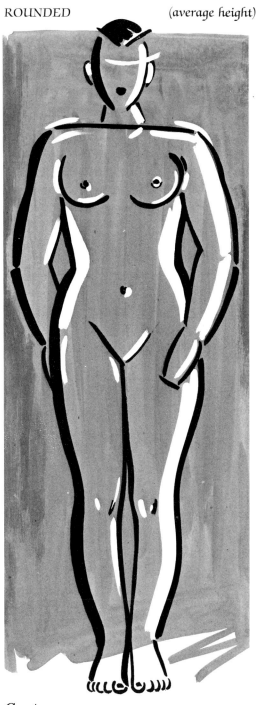

★ V-necks also flatter a big bust and a round face.

★ High necklines, scarves and chokers flatter a long neck.

★ Long strings of beads, scarves and polo necks balance a thicker neck.

★ Crew necks are softened when combined with shirts or scarves.

Shoulder Lines

★ Batwing, raglan and kimono sleeves all balance broad shoulders, as do V-neck tops.

★ Square necklines, puff sleeves and epaulettes flatter narrow shoulders.
   If you must wear shoulder pads, make sure they are small.

★ Dropped shoulder styles emphasise the natural line of the shoulder.

★ A squared shoulder line flatters narrow shoulders and a large bust. Inset styles are flattering to nearly all figures.

Skirts

★ On-the-knee lengths flatter most people.

★ Very full and very long skirts should only be worn by tall girls.

★ Short skirts look best on youthful bodies!

★ Pleated skirts emphasise wide hips.

★ Softer and fuller skirts can be slimming.

Legs

Short legs require the balance of shorter jackets. They can look longer if you wear separates of the same or toning colours. Avoid dramatic colour contrasts. Large legs look bigger in cropped trousers and calf-length skirts.

Trousers

★ Generally, trousers are more flattering in smooth fabrics for instance, jersey, gaberdine, silk or flannel.

SLIGHT

Layers (although not too bulky) can look attractive, giving an illusion of added volume. Avoid garments which cling tightly, these will exaggerate a slender frame. Keep clear of vertical lines which will make this shape look thinner.

AVERAGE

Emphasise and elongate your body through the clothes you wear. This shape can wear a wide variety of looks -- make the most of it.

ROUNDED

If in doubt, go one size up – tight clothes don't look so good on you. Don't wear extreme lengths or shapes. Look for fluid, slightly looser, flattering lines.

Coats

★ Double breasted, tailored styles are slimming.

★ Belted coats do not usually suit smaller ladies.

Necklines

★ Soft cowl and V-necks lengthen the neck.

BUILDING ON THE BASICS

Petite, yet with ample bosom. An easy shape to flatter as long as care is taken to avert attention from the bust in order to elongate the overall shape. Avoid lines finishing at the bust line, or clothes with lots of detail in this area.

Tall and thin. Pattern and bolder shape can help balance and enhance this shape. Avoid high heels. Layers can be most flattering if used wisely and not to excess.

Pear shaped. Discreet padding of shoulders and minimal 'squaring' of shape through well chosen garments can successfully balance this bottom-heavy shape.

Rounded, taller than average. Dress confidently and boldly. Avoid frills and flounces; keep to simple lines which skim and are slightly looser over any particular problem areas.

Sweaters

★ Mohairs and chunky and heavily textured yarns will swamp small people and emphasise size if you are large.

★ Cropped shapes will emphasise the waist.

★ Long tubular sweaters minimise a large bust.

★ Polo necks should be avoided by people with short necks.

Shape and fashion

The emphasis of scale, proportion and balance is changing in quite a dramatic way. We are moving away from the harsh, angular lines of 'power dressing' towards a much softer and more flexible silhouette. The body is being emphasised in a relaxed way and exaggerated shapes are seen less often.

Designers are using more feminine fabrics such as chiffons, georgettes and stretch jerseys to create a wide variety of styles. Waists are often understated, hips are more defined and sometimes swathed, skirts come in an assortment of lengths and are often draped. This more flexible approach to fashion means that it will be much easier for every figure type to find flattering and comfortable clothes.

Whatever the fashion, it is always essential to be aware of the proportions of the look you are creating. For instance, if you are wearing a short top you may want to team it with a longer, draped skirt. Flat or low-heeled shoes and bold yet minimal jewellery will complete the look. This is balance. Similarly, a hip-length jacket worn with a skirt to the knee will require flat or higher shoes. Styling, co-ordinating and accessorising are vitally important. As soon as you add some jewellery, take away a scarf, slot in a new bag or a different height of heel, you subtly alter the balance. You do not have to follow fashion blindly – just be aware of shifting trends and be prepared to make a few adjustments.

Sizing

Size varies dramatically from manufacturer to manufacturer and from shop to shop. Modern factory techniques can create variations in identical garments. Be prepared for your size to vary. As a standard size 12 you may find that sizes 10 and 14 also fit you, depending on the designer or manufacturer.

Shops do not always stock a full range of sizes for every style, so you may find that the garment that you want is not available in your size. Stock is decided by which clothes are best suited to which size. Tight, short dresses are going to look far better on smaller women and, equally, loosely cut styles tend to be favoured by larger women.

Take note of which designer's clothes fit you well. Often, a fashion designer can have great ideas for petite women, but does not translate these ideas so well for tall or larger women. Most designers are designing for themselves. It makes sense, therefore, that their clothes will not suit all shapes and sizes.

Shop around until you find a label, a name or a shop which caters for your shape and your taste.

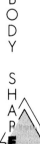

SIZES

BRITISH	EUROPEAN	AMERICAN
8	36	6
10	38	8
12	40	10
14	42	12
16	44	14
18	46	16
20	48	18

BUST SIZES

BRITISH/AMERICAN	EUROPEAN
32 in	76cm
34 in	78cm
36 in	80cm
38 in	82cm
40 in	84cm
42 in	86cm
44 in	88cm
46 in	90cm

SHOES SIZES

BRITISH	EUROPEAN	AMERICAN
3	36	4 ½
4	37	5 ½
5	38	6 ½
6	39	7 ½
7	40	8 ½
8	41	9 ½
9	42	10 ½
10	43	11 ½

Shape and history

As we all know, concepts of beauty have changed completely over the centuries. We have come a long way from Botticelli, Titian and Goya's voluptuous temptresses cavorting on canvas. We have hurtled through the Twentieth century, witnessing extra-ordinary changes in our society's perception of beauty and the 'perfect' figure. We have veered from tiny waists and enormous bustles, to poor Miss Great Britain of the Twenties, with her flattened, boyish breasts. On through the languid Thirties, with a slight hint of soft, womanly curves returning, to the Forties and the strictness and disciplines of wartime. The Fifties was the era of 'youth', with curvy and cute teenagers. Miss Sixties was forced onto a crash diet, in order to conform to the era's penchant for stick insect figures. The Seventies look is not so easy to define. Now, we have hit the tough, hard Eighties, where fit, lean, strong bodies reflect our struggles in the male dominated board room.

What we must remember is that although fashions in beauty and in women's shapes constantly change, our basic figures do not! Women are still, fundamentally, the same shape as they were a hundred years ago. Diet and exercise will, of course, make you leaner, but they cannot alter your fundamental shape, which is governed by genetics. My advice is, therefore, to learn to like your figure, and to make the best of it, whatever the 'fashion'.

Dangerous distortions

The pressures exerted on women by society to conform to shape stereotypes can be very powerful, leading to thousands of women feeling a total loss of self-confidence. Even worse, more and more women are developing eating disorders such as anorexia and bulimia. These dreadful – often fatal – diseases are sometimes a direct result of our unrealistic expectations of what women should look like.

CHAPTER THREE

Colour

★ A colour update ★

★ Base and complementary colours ★

★ Seasonal colour ★

★ Patterns ★

★ Make-up ★

When choosing the colours of your clothes, the main element to consider is your own colouring – your skin, your hair and your eyes. This is even more important than colour co-ordination within your wardrobe. You should ensure that the tones which you wear are not too similar to your skin and hair. Equally, colour should not be so strong that it dominates you.

Our climate, the light and our surroundings also have a large bearing upon the shades that look good on us. A vivid turquoise which looks fabulous in the golden light of the Mediterranean, may not have the same impact on a grey summer's day in England.

Last, but by no means least, your personality plays a major role in the success of the colours which you wear. If you are shy and retiring, neither you or those around you, will be able to cope with you daubed in dazzling prints. If you are a wild extrovert, you will send out very confusing messages if you are clad in an unobtrusive beige.

Colour mistakes can often be summed up by those unworn items of clothing which we all have tucked away in our wardrobes. Have a good look at one of them. It is difficult to pinpoint why you are loath to wear it. You really don't mind the style. Have another look. Perhaps it is the colour which is not quite right – too loud; too subtle; the pattern is too dazzling? It would be fabulous on a sun kissed beach, but, let's face it – it's a winter garment! We all make mistakes with colour because there are no hard and fast rules to follow. You have to learn through experience.

A colour update

When planning the interior of your home, you think very carefully about colour schemes and co-ordinating the shades and tones of each room. Your wardrobe should be approached in exactly the same manner, the main difference being that you are unlikely to throw out all your clothes and start from scratch. It is, however, possible to gradually develop your existing wardrobe so that you shift the emphasis of colours as the seasons progress. Your clothes will immediately be given a new lease of life.

Base and complementary colours

A closer examination of what is hanging in your wardrobe will reveal BASE and COMPLEMENTARY colours. You will, no doubt, have several garments in one or two main colours. These colours are likely to be black, brown, navy, denim, grey, camel or sand. These are your BASE colours. The remainder of your clothes are probably a mixture of assorted colours – your COMPLEMENTARY colours – which should work well with the BASE colours. You now have to learn how to successfully mix the two groups; how to co-ordinate the colours to their full advantage.

For the last several years, black has been the main base colour. Indeed, it has totally dominated thousands of wardrobes! More recently, black has been broken up and made less sombre with splashes of brights and primary colours. There is now a gradual shift away from black as a base colour. Brown, navy, claret, aubergine, pine and shades of grey are being used more and more as colour foundations.

The full cast of supporting or complementary colours which successfully work with the new base colours, emerges as a whole new spectrum. Shades of earth, terracotta, spice, paprika, ginger and cinnamon look wonderful when toned with brown as a base colour. Alternatively, they can be

used to contrast pine or grey. Aqua, china and powder blue and dusty pinks can all be used as complementary colours with matt brown, dark navy or grey bases.

Seasonal colour

As the seasons progress, the emphasis of the colour spectrums gradually shifts, evolving alongside new textures and new lines.

Colours are greatly determined by our climate which does not have clearly defined or predictable seasons. We do not suddenly switch from summer to winter clothes. Our seasons gradually run into each other with quite lengthy periods when we are combining winter with spring and summer with autumn.

Whatever new base colours are introduced for winter, they will always tend to be heavy – browns and deep shades of green for instance. Summer bases will be lighter – cream, tan or stone. Summer bases can be combined with toning colours or you can choose splashes of complete contrast to complement and accentuate the base colour.

Learning about colour trends

It is important to develop an awareness of colour and colour trends. In this way you will learn how to distinguish between lasting developments and short-lived fads. Have a look through the glossy monthly magazines which carry reports about the new designer collections each season. The newspapers will also discuss colour trends when the designer shows are on. Television is covering style more extensively too. Many designer shops show videos of their shows – go and have a look. Although it is impossible for most women to attend the fashion shows, it is becoming easier and easier to gather the relevant information.

Colour changes usually take place at the more expensive end of the market first. Even if you cannot afford to buy the clothes, it is well worth taking note of what is going on in that area. Remember what you see because sooner, rather than later, some of the colour influences will reach the high street. You will then be in a good position to shop more shrewdly.

If you do not feel inclined to jump in head first, try dipping one toe in! Experiment with accessories in a new shade, followed by a new make-up colour. These touches are a good way of introducing a new colour without breaking the bank. You will give the impression that you are aware of the

COLOUR OPTIONS

Traditional base colours can be teamed with complementary shades and tones in the classic way. Alternatively, base colours which are currently popular can be matched with fresh tones. The colour choices you make will depend on you: your taste, mood, style, personality and the feel that you have for colour. But here are some ideas to get you thinking. Choose a palette and have a go!

current colour trends. More importantly, you will not be taking fashion too seriously – it is great fun to dabble!

Patterns

Patterns are inevitably linked with the fabrics which you like and the textures which you feel comfortable wearing. There are certain guidelines, related to your size and shape, which should be followed. Just as bulky fabrics will add to your size, so will bold patterns. If you are larger, try using colour to enhance your shape, rather than choosing big, abstract patterns. As always, detract from problem areas, and draw attention to your assets!

By all means, use pattern for areas which you want to be noticed. For example if the upper part of your body is fairly trim, then you can let rip with a boldly patterned top. Balance your shape and the overall look with a self-coloured, preferably darker colour which will frame you and give the illusion of slimness if you are 'bottom heavy'. Simply reverse the process if your problem is a large bust and waist.

Remember that small patterns help to 'frame' the body, whereas large, flamboyant patterns visually add to size.

Wearing a pattern is a wonderful way of breaking up solid colour, accessorising, or simply adding interest to more sombre tones. It can make or break an outfit. Used badly, colour can cause utter confusion to anyone witnessing the wild chaos displayed on a body. Well co-ordinated pattern, combined with a plain colour is fabulous.

If you want to see colour and patterns superbly used, take a look at the work of Kenzo, who has successfully combined exciting patterns in vivid colours for over twenty years. With his distinctive, bold style of patterning, even the most basic greys and browns come alive. His prints are instantly recognisable, and his influence seeps right through to the high street shops.

Make-up

When you are introducing new colours into your wardrobe, it is essential to reassess your lip and eye colours.

Colour co-ordination in your make-up is just as important as for your clothes and it should be considered alongside your clothes to create a total look, even for everyday wear. Choose subtle shades which will complement the new colour trends.

Remember that make-up for the day should be subtle whereas make-up for the evening worn in artificial light can afford to be much stronger and more dramatic.

Natural colour

Apart from complementing your clothes, make-up should also complement your natural colouring. You want colour to work for you to enhance your natural attributes.

The suggestions for lip and eye colours below are linked to your hair colour – whether it is natural or artificial. Remember, within these categories there are infinite variations. Most people can wear most colours if they are imaginatively applied and worn with appropriate clothes. Basically, there are no rules. Enjoy yourself – try some new shades. Colour gives us enthusiasm and energy!

Blond Hair

Daytime Colours: Delicate, pastel shades will complement your colouring. Use palest pink, powder blue, hints of cream, soft brown or pale grey for the eyes. Continue the theme with shades of pink through to brown/beige tones for the lips. Avoid orange tints.

Evening Colours: Blondes can become vamps! Darken your eyes with smoke grey or brown. Balance the eye colour with fuschia, plum or light scarlet lips. Avoid using contrasting colours on the eyes and the lips – they will swamp you.

Red Hair

Daytime Colours: With a stronger hair colour, you can choose pastel palettes, or a deeper, contrasting look. Try pale lavender, silver or turquoise on your eyes, or go for more impact with darker tones of grey, apricot, rust, brown, blue or green. Balance paler eye make-up with sugar pink lips or, to complement darker eyes, try richer tones of peach, copper, terracotta, beige, brown, rust, scarlet or dark red.

Evening Colours: Take this opportunity to emphasise all your assets! Use deeper shades of your daytime colours, using only one or two shades at the same time. Your hair is a potent colour feature in itself, so keep your make-up strong and simple.

Brown Hair

Daytime Colours: Brunettes look great wearing classical brown or grey eye colours. Lipstick should be subtle – most tones of pink, beige and brown can be worn, but be wary of orange or cerise. If you want a stronger lip colour choose scarlet, dark red or rust, remembering to keep the eye colour simple.

Evening Colours: Play the vamp with dark eye colours and dramatic lips. Alternatively, try purple, lavender or violet eyes with paler lipsticks in shades of lavender or pink. These colours are particularly effective with brown, navy or taupe clothes. As always, avoid mixing too many eye

and lip colours at a time. The result will not look attractive or complement your clothes.

Black Hair

Daytime Colours: You can, very effectively, create a 'pale and interesting' look with very subtle colours, or you can go for a stronger effect with dark grey or brown eye colours and deep lipsticks. Remember that your hair colour is very dramatic, so be careful. You do not want to end up looking painted.

Evening Colours: If you have a pale skin, blue or green eye colours can look fabulous. Lips can remain pale to balance subtle eye make-up, or a bold splash or scarlet, rust or burgundy can look very dramatic with your colouring.

Using eye shadows

Avoid using eye shadow which does not complement the colour of your eyes. For instance, blue eye shadow does not look good next to green eyes (and vice versa) and mauve does not complement green or blue eyes, unless the tone is very carefully selected.

As well as thinking about your hair and your clothes, your skin tone should also be considered before applying make-up. Certain shades of lipstick and eye colour complement certain skin tones. For instance, people with ruddy complexions should not over-emphasise their healthy look with lots of pinks, oranges or reds. Apricot, gold and amethyst eye colours nearly always look good on black skin, and pale people should use colour – whatever shade it is – in moderation.

CHAPTER FOUR

Planning Your Wardrobe

★ The big clear-out ★

★ Styling ★

★ Studying the classics ★

★ Essential looks ★

★ Underneath it all ★

★ Accessories ★

Do not be fooled by the idea that lots of fashion is short-lived and throw-away. Clothes are too expensive for this attitude. You do not change your sitting room decor every six months — you would expect it to last several years, allowing for a few adjustments here and there. Clothes should be treated in exactly the same way. Creating a wardrobe is a major investment and requires a clear, organised approach.

Having digested the earlier sections about shape and colour, you will now have a good idea of which clothes you look best in. You will also have gained the confidence to wear them. It is now time for 'the big clear-out'. You need to take a good look at your clothes and accessories and to spend some time re-organising them. It is a laborious process, but worth it. Once this stage is complete, we are going to learn about 'styling', which is the professional term used for putting it all together. With a little bit of know-how, you will be amazed at just how many looks you can achieve with the clothes at your disposal. Most garments can be worn in several different ways — it is up to you to decide precisely how.

The big clear-out

What you are aiming to do is to achieve a 'working' wardrobe — a wardrobe which works for you! In order to succeed, you have to be positive. We often become very sentimental about certain items in the wardrobe. We hoard lots of useless, out-of-date garments 'just-in-case'.

Take everything out of the wardrobe, including all the oddments from the back of the cupboard. Remove all the items that you have collected over the years from the drawers. Take a thorough and critical look at what you now have in front of you.

The first decision to be made is which clothes you want to keep. This is a good time to enlist the help of a very close friend — he or she will be able to be far more objective than you. Decide which garments are useful: do you wear them frequently, sometimes, or not at all? This will enable you to pinpoint the items which have lost any relevance within your wardrobe. Quite a good criterion is to dispose of any garments which have not seen the light of day for two years, or more. Pile up the sales mistakes alongside the wrong colours which you had intentions of dyeing, the out-of-date horrors and any items which are too small. Be brave! Refrain from lobbing ANYTHING back into the wardrobe which is not of use, otherwise you have completely wasted your time.

If there are nearly new 'reject' garments, take them to a charity shop or give the odd garment to a friend who has expressed enthusiasm over it — it might look better on her than it did on you! If you have unearthed expensive, unworn garments, try selling them in a designer second-time-around shop. Stack any items that you are unsure about into a suitcase or trunk.

Now apply the same process — just as ruthlessly — to your shoes and accessories.

You will find that you are left with a nucleus of garments and accessories which you like, which suit you and which you enjoy wearing. These items will form the basis of your new wardrobe. The choice is simpler, the look is stronger, and you can clearly see where the gaps are.

Perfect timing

Your wardrobe clear-out should be scheduled for the very end of a season — preferably summer. This will enable you to clear the decks and get organised before the winter when the bulk of more expensive buying is done.

Styling

The next stage is to sort out the mass of clothing and accessories into sections which are relevant to your lifestyle, for instance: work, sports activities, taking the children to school, lunches, formal dinner parties and so on.

Within the fashion industry — magazines, newspapers, and fashion shows — a 'stylist' is employed to co-ordinate each look. The stylist is responsible for choosing the clothes to create the desired image, and then accessorising them.

Let us take an example. A fashion magazine editor plans a fashion feature and decides that the theme will be a sporty, 'colonial' daytime look for spring. The stylist will choose tailored, crisp sand-coloured clothes to fit the theme. The garments will consist of jodpurs and Fifties-style tapered slacks, tailored shirts in cotton drill buttoned to the neck, pleated skirts and jackets with epaulettes, pockets and brass buttons. To accessorise the garments she will use cotton military style caps or berets, sturdy tan-coloured leather belts, flat tan lace-up or loafer shoes, tan leather binocular cases or attaché cases, tan string-back leather gloves. There will be little or no jewellery except, perhaps, a watch. The models' make-up will consist of brownish eye make-up and darker lips. Their hair will be straight, shiny and simple if it is short, plaited or tied back if it is longer.

If it is decided that this 'colonial' look should be softer and more feminine, the same colour theme and clothes will be used, but the military lines are softened. Shirts are opened at the neck; a cream chiffon scarf is tossed around the shoulders; skirts are softened with more feminine belts; a fabulous straw or Panama hat may be added; lighter and more lady-like sandals with a low heel are added;

string or lace gloves are used; a soft squashy shoulder bag may be added. The jewellery will definitely be pearl and/or gold. The eye make-up will be lighter and subtly emphasised by natural lips and nails. Whatever the length of hair, it will be softer with some movement.

As you can see, every detail is carefully planned. From a basic pile of garments, the stylist is expected to be able to create a multitude of different looks. The same principles can be applied to your own wardrobe. It requires time, a cool, clear eye and a certain amount of flexibility in looking at your clothes afresh and trying different combinations.

Work through your wardrobe, section by section, beginning with your casual wear. Hang all your tops — shirts, sweaters and sweatshirts — on a rail and lay out all the bottoms below them. Decide which garments look good together. There will be several items which you will want to wear in the usual way, but do not be complacent. Try restyling these favourites, too. You will find new uses for garments which you have always

TAKE ONE JACKET

CLASSIC

FEMININE

SPORTY

STYLISED

It is easy to vary the way a basic garment can be worn. An everyday jacket can be imaginatively styled to create lots of different looks. As style ideas come and go, it is useful to learn the knack of 'accessorising' differently. It just takes a spot of confidence.

liked but which you had never managed to team with anything successfully.

Having had a preliminary run through the various sections of your wardrobe, the items must be tried on to see which of your new ideas work and how they can be accessorised to develop the look further. Not all the combinations will be successful — be prepared to re-jig and re-match.

Have a good look at your shoes, belts, bags, hats and jewellery and team them with your new 'looks'. Again, be flexible. Try putting a different belt on a favourite pair of trousers. What about accessorising an everyday dress with more dramatic jewellery? Perhaps you need to adjust the height of heel that you are wearing with a certain skirt length, or you should try a shorter, cropped jacket with a longer skirt. Remember that balance and proportion are essential, whatever the outfit.

Styling is an invaluable exercise in making your wardrobe 'work' for you. You will now have a clear indication of the clothes which you definitely need to buy to complete the images.

Studying the classics

As a vital part of smarter daytime dressing as well as informal evening looks, it is a good idea to learn how to make the best use of 'classic' items of dress. You will, no doubt, have discovered some of the following items in the depths of your wardrobe: a tweed hacking jacket; a blazer or wool jacket; a trench coat; a white silk blouse; jodpurs or breeches; a long-length pleated skirt; a straight knee-length skirt; a trouser or skirt suit. These are all 'classics' and can prove to be very useful. Even if you do not normally buy these types of clothes, look for the current styling of these important garments. Look through fashion magazines to see how similar garments are currently being shown by couture houses. You will probably be able to adapt your own 'classics' to create a more directional image.

How the designers do it

Yves St Laurent regularly makes good use of navy fine wool or gaberdine blazers which are often trimmed with gilt naval-style buttons. He favours long lean lines. Georgio Armani frequently plays with check and tweed jackets for a softer, more sporty classic. The American designer, Ralph Lauren is renowned for his styling of British traditional looks. He regularly teams riding trousers with fabulous tweed jackets, polo necks or shirts.

Many designers play with the classics, styling them afresh to give them a new slant. Britain's Ally Capellino has done this successfully, creating looks which are evocative of Agatha Christie's Miss Marples. Vivienne Westwood has translated British classics 'regally' in her own inimitable way. It is well worth seeing what designers are doing. You can then buy less expensively and style the garments as you wish.

Wearing the classics

The Blazer is one of the most flattering and versatile of garments. It teams easily with wider trousers, with or without turn-ups, slim, simple knee-length skirts and longer pleated skirts. It looks best with a fine, round-neck top underneath. Blazer jackets can be found in many high street shops and can often be inexpensively bought second-hand. Men's shops are another source of good quality blazers. Navy is the most versatile and suitable base colour for this garment.

The Tweed Jacket is a softer version of the blazer. It looks best in fine fabrics with beige, rust, brown or grey base colours and a soft peplum. Team the jacket with wide trousers, a knee-length wrap skirt or a long, soft skirt. A soft, flimsy blouse underneath will balance the look.

Jodphurs can be bought as a fashion item or in sports shops. For everyday wear, it is wisest to choose a stretch fabric in a style which is not skin-tight. Riding trousers look great when teamed with hacking jackets. You may, however, find that this look is too strong, in which case you will get lots of wear out of these clothes if they are worn separately.

Trench Coats looks best when they are tossed on nonchalantly! The style should be of ample proportions in size and length. For durability, buy a coat with a detachable lining. You can then unclip the lining in the spring and throw on your trench coat as an extra layer. It is worth investing in a good quality, fairly fine fabric such as cotton poplin or gaberdine, as a trench coat is a true classic which will last you for many years.

The Classic Blouse is one of the most feminine garments you can wear. It looks best when it is worn very simply with a minimum of accessories. If you want the garment to last for years without dating, choose a simple style with minimal detailing. A white blouse looks fabulous in fine cotton, and wonderful in silk.

Peg-top Trousers should be in flannel or gaberdine, and can be with or without turn-ups. Avoid fabrics which are too bulky or heavy – they do not look good and they feel awful to wear. These trousers must fit immaculately. Choose a neutral colour such as navy, grey, camel, black or brown which you can team easily with other garments.

The Pleated Skirt should also be in a neutral colour and of a medium weight, good quality fabric. Classics

always look more chic when presented in a neutral colour.

The Knee-length Skirt has to fit extremely well. Teamed with the classic blouse and one of the classic jackets, it can look fabulous.

The Suit must fit beautifully and be manufactured in a high quality fabric. Team it with a blouse, some stunning, simple jewellery and a chic pair of classic court shoes and you have an exquisite, enduring look which will see you through countless more formal occasions.

Be imaginative with your classics. Perhaps you could team a classic jacket which you already have with a new skirt, or a wider, floppy pair of trousers. Have a search through your partner's wardrobe – perhaps he has a wonderful waistcoat to complement the look. Have you always worn your blazer with the sleeves rolled up, combined with a sweatshirt and a gathered skirt? Now is the time to try it understated, sticking to clean, sharp lines. Try it with a fine, classic sweater and a slimline skirt. There are lots of possible variations – be adventurous.

Each of these classics can prove to be invaluable for evening wear. The blazer or jacket can look stunning with the addition of chunkier earrings and a large brooch to give a stronger look. The silk blouse can look fabulous with a string of pearls or a soft, chiffon scarf knotted around the neck for added softness and feminity. The trousers will look extremely chic just by adding a simple belt.

Essential looks

When planning your wardrobe, it is essential to have a clear idea of the purpose of each outfit that you are creating and how it will slot into your

TAKING A LOOK AT THE CLASSICS

BLAZER

Classic garments
are invaluable.
Good quality,
more simply
tailored
garments last
longer and date
less quickly. They
are easy to mix
and match,
slotting in
comfortably
alongside more
current ideas.

PLANNING YOUR WARDROBE

PLEAT
SKIRT

TRENCH
COAT

WIDE-LEG
TROUSERS

Whether you are buying or making a garment, the type of fabric that you choose is as important as the style of the clothing. Look at the fabric, and feel it – does it crease easily in your hand? Does it feel too rough to wear or too flimsy to hang properly? When you try a garment on, linger for a few minutes to get the feel of the fabric. It should be so comfortable that you are almost unaware of it. If it feels heavy or itchy, think again, however good the garment looks. The care of the garment must also be considered, so read the care label before buying anything. New sophisticated fabrics, incorporating both man-made and natural fibres are introduced every season. Lycra, for instance, whether blended with silk, cotton, or used on its own, has revolutionised the fabric industry. The following chart gives you the qualities of basic dress-making fabrics. Armed with this information, and the wisdom of your experience, you will be able to shop more wisely.

NATURAL FABRICS

Cotton

Cotton is manufactured in an enourmous variety of weights and weaves. Calico, damask, canvas, lawn, poplin, voile, muslin and towelling are all woven out of cotton. Lace and jersey are also often made from this natural material. Cotton is ideal for summer clothing because it allows the body to breathe and perspire freely, making it comfortable and easy to wear. It is also hard-wearing and can usually be thrown into the washing machine without too much thought. One of the charms of this relatively inexpensive fabric is that, whatever weight or weave it is produced in, it always has a 'fresh' look.

Cotton's obvious drawback is that is creases easily. It is for this reason that it is woven into 'sweat' fabrics, and blended with man-made fibres such as lycra, to produce a variety of sophisticated fabrics.

Linen

This expensive fabric, which is woven from flax, is a perennial favourite with most designers. Pure linen creases very badly – you only have to sit down for a few minutes, and the garment looks as if you have been sleeping in it – but this is part of its charm! Man-made fibres are sometimes blended with linen to produce a fabric which does not crease so easily. However, a lot of the material's unique appeal is also lost. Pure linen hangs beautifully, whereas mixes are often stiff or too flimsy.

Silk

Made from the fine threads produced by silkworms, silk is used to produce a vast range of beautiful fabics including chiffon, lace, velvet, voile, tulle, taffeta, as well as slubbed silks such as shantung. The luxurious qualities of silk, make it an ideal fabric for evening clothes. Generally speaking, the better quality of the silk, the more hard wearing and easy to care for it will be. However, many silks have to be dry-cleaned, so read the care label before buying.

Wool

Wool is used to produce a large variety of weights and weaves of fabric, from very light, fine jersey to the heavy, 'felty' fabrics which are used to make thick winter clothes. Wool is often blended with man-made fibres, to produce cheaper fabrics but, if you can afford it, it is always worth investing in good-quality pure-wool garments for winter. Not only do they look and feel wonderful to wear, they will last for years.

MAN-MADE FABRICS

Lycra

Lycra is used when garments need to be body-hugging. It has revolutionised the underwear trade and beautiful, figure-skimming styles are now produced from lycra and silk weaves. It is also widely used for swimwear to manufacture cotton/lycra swimsuits which cling to the body, while still allowing the skin to breathe. Although lycra is hard-wearing, garments containing this material should, generally speaking, be hand-washed.

Nylon

This once-popular fabric (remember 'drip-dry' shirts?) is no longer considered to be very stylish, and the fact that the skin cannot breathe through it, makes it clammy to wear. It is, however, cheap and hard-wearing.

Polyester

This relatively cheap material is produced in a variety of guises. It is used to successfully imitate natural fibres such as silk and cotton. However, it does not allow your skin to breathe freely and is, therefore, uncomfortable to wear in hot weather. Very easy to wash and care for, polyester is often blended with natural fibres to make them easier to care for, as well as less expensive to manufacture.

lifestyle. It is not worth throwing on all your best clothes to visit the supermarket or getting dressed up to take the children to school. The clothes will get spoiled and you will gain a reputation as being vaguely eccentric! Wear the garment for the purpose – your clothes will last much longer and you will feel more confident.

Casual clothes

Nothing can beat cotton sweatshirt fabric for softness and comfort. It stretches with your body and feels wonderful. You need a selection of tracksuits or tops and track pants to mix and match, using your new-found awareness of colour co-ordination. You can wear them around the home and around the town during the day. A word of warning: it is very easy to disguise extra weight under this style of clothing. Make sure that you are not gradually expanding under that comfortable, stretchy tracksuit.

Formal daytime clothes

Lunches with friends, social calls and certain daytime appointments are all occasions when it is important for you to put across a stylish, relaxed image which will make you feel good and, therefore, project yourself better. The person you are meeting will appreciate it. This involves creating a simple, comfortable and stylish look. Clothes in this range should be easy to throw on – skirt and trouser suits, dresses and jackets can all be worn. Accessories play a larger part and will need more co-ordination. Your shoes, gloves and bag should all work together. Jewellery should be used to accentuate the style but it must not be too 'flashy'. Your hair and make-up should be slick. What about a touch of perfume? Do not overdo any aspect of this style of dressing, or the effect will be ruined. Pay attention to detail and spend extra time grooming yourself to achieve a chic, finished result.

Informal evening wear

Drinks, parties and discos offer a wonderful opportunity to dress up for the evening. It is fun and friends will respond favourably to the fact that you have made an effort. Everyone loves being in the company of a pretty woman. 'Social' clothing should feature in your wardrobe along with your other sections. A more feminine look, featuring a lot of dresses, is becoming more popular, perhaps running parallel with the new morality of the Nineties. You can afford to emphasise your hair, make-up and accessories because artificial light dilutes colour.

Underneath it all

Has your wardrobe clear-out revealed grey, dingy knickers and bras? If so throw them out! Well-fitting, attractive underwear is essential for a totally stylish look – and it will make you feel much more confident.

The development of fine stretch fabrics and trimmings has completely revolutionised underwear over the last few years. Colours are more tempting than ever. There is often a vast, baffling choice available in department stores. Many women are buying their underwear in smaller, local lingerie shops which usually stock lovely, chic ranges.

Underwear extras
Never buy knickers which are too small. Go one size up if necessary. Visible panti-lines look hideous!
★
Avoid lumps under fine clothing by cutting the labels out of your underwear. It is more comfortable, too.
★
Never wear a black bra under a white T-shirt or blouse, or vice versa. It looks most unattractive.

THE LITTLE BLACK DRESS

'ROMANCE'

Romantic and feminine – the perfect ballgown for a formal occasion. Make most impact by softening the look with delicate jewellery and accessories. Simple satin shoes look fabulous with an evening dress.

'FIFTIES'

P L A N N I N G   Y O U R   W A R D R O B E

Carry this look through by wearing stilettoes and period marcasite or diamante jewellery. Alternatively, balance the look with 'current' jewellery and flat pumps.

'LATIN'

Fun, daring and easy to wear. Make sure that you keep it simple – earrings will add all the drama you need.

'BODY HUGGING'

The main essentials for this look are a good body and wonderful legs! Make sure that your tights are perfect – opaque give the best effect. Shoes should be simple – choose flat pumps or low-to-mid heels. Jewellery should be bold and/or stark.

Shoestring black looks

Those of you who like the idea of 'the little black dress', should read on! If you cannot afford to spend a lot on this item, it really is worth having a look through the less expensive stores. Most retailers carry a reasonably priced version of it. Cleverly accessorised, it will look a million dollars! If the dress is for a special, one-off occasion, hiring is another solution. You may save a great deal of money in terms of avoiding mad panics, impulse buys and later regrets. If you are lucky enough to have a dress-maker in the family, patterns have improved enormously over the past few years. Having secured your 'little black dress' you will find that it is very versatile. There are countless ways in which you can style it. Try stark and bare with a cashmere cardigan and no jewellery; a string of pearls; a locket on a chic black ribbon – the possibilities are endless.

Buying a bra

The first step is to be measured. It is essential to make sure that the cup size is right. Wrongly sized underwired bras can be bad for you and short straps can cause bruises and ridges on your shoulders. Always try on bras, even if you have bought the make before. Manufacturers' sizes vary, as do your breasts throughout your life. Choose a bra to suit your shape. If you have a large bust, there is an extensive selection of support bras to choose from. For those with small busts smooth, padded and stretch bras are available, as well as underwired bras with detachable padding. You must also consider the purpose that you are buying it for − is it for sport, everyday wear, to emphasise your shape or for tight-fitting clothes? The style that you buy will depend upon the role that it is destined to play.

Knickers!

Try some of the deeper, larger shapes for everyday wear and for trousers. They are much more flattering than 'bikini' styles and much more comfortable. Treat yourself to some feminine lacy knickers to match your wonderful new bra. G-strings are strictly for mid summer and for those in fabulous shape! They do, however, dispense with the visible panti-line problem under sheer or tight clothes.

A smoother outline

Body-stockings and body-shapers give a wonderfully improved silhouette enabling us to smooth out areas where, previously, there were tell-tale lumps and bumps; places where unyielding bras ended and knickers with tight elastic started or finished. They are a must under any garment which clings. On the other hand, if you are wearing softer, looser clothes, nothing can beat the luxury of silk camisoles or camiknickers next to your skin.

Accessories

Accessories are a stylist's tools of the trade. They can completely alter the 'look' of any outfit. Invest as much as you possibly can in a few good quality, basic accessories. They will look better, adding style to cheaper clothes, and they will last longer. Eventually, this will allow you to allocate more of your budget to clothes, rather than constantly replacing basic accessories.

When planning your wardrobe, the easiest way is to list the essential accessories that you will need to complete your outfits. These are the minimum accessories that you will need to form the backbone of your wardrobe.

Shoes: Black or brown flat walking shoes; a pair of sports shoes, for instance trainers; black medium heels for more dressy wear. Anything else is optional.

Belts: One black leather belt; one brown leather belt; a softer more delicate belt, perhaps in suede, for evening wear.

Bags: A fairly large shoulder bag in a neutral colour and/or a brief-case, music or attache case in black or brown. For the evening, a small evening purse in black suede or leather.

Gloves: During the winter you will need two pairs of gloves – one hardwearing sturdy leather pair in a neutral colour for everyday wear and a more chic pair in fine, soft leather for the evening and special occasions.

Jewellery: This is a matter of individual choice. Fairly chunky costume jewellery in 'gold' or silver is very useful and versatile.

Apart from the basic items listed above you will, no doubt, collect scarves, hats, tights and lots of other extras which are useful for styling your clothes. When you make any of these purchases, bear in mind how they will 'work'. It is all too easy to waste money on extras which turn out to be completely useless.

One of the most important guidelines on styling is to avoid looking as if you are wearing either national costume or fancy dress. Only the under thirties can risk it, if they are daring!

We will now look at your basic accessories in more detail.

Shoes

Shoes provide BALANCE to any outfit and play an enormous part in the success, or failure, of a 'look'. The heel height, toe shape and trimming are crucial in balancing the length of a skirt, a jacket or the cut of a pair of trousers. Your shoes make it obvious whether you are going for a 'current' look or not and are an instant way of revamping an old garment. Do remember to polish them regularly and to rest them whenever possible – they will look better and will also last much longer.

Belts

Belts are another important styling

touch. Look in magazines and more directional shops to see how belts are being used – is the focus on the hips or on the waist? Note whether heavy or more delicate designs are in vogue and pay attention to buckles and fastenings. There are always a multitude of belts to choose from in the shops, from fancy medieval styles to cowboy belts and classics. Observe the ways in which designers and stylists are currently using belts and create your own style.

Bags

Bags complete an outfit and should, therefore, match your shoes and your belt. If possible, choose good quality, soft leather. Shoulder bags are by far the most popular and useful of styles for daywear, although there are lots of interesting alternatives available. Avoid the temptation of continually throwing bits and pieces into your bag. Its shape will soon be ruined and it will become a dead weight to carry. Be strict with yourself, and empty non-essential items out. For the evening, restrict yourself to carrying a small leather or plain fabric purse to contain your lipstick, powder, handkerchief and some money. It looks more feminine and helps to co-ordinate your look.

Jewellery

Jewellery is a very personal matter. A lot of women enjoy collecting gold, pearls, and classic rings with precious stones. Real jewellery always looks dainty and feminine, its only disadvantage being that it is finer and

STYLE STORIES

Accessories are used to create a complete look. Bags, belts, jewellery and all the other pieces which you team with your clothes help to co-ordinate the garments which you wear. When accessorising, think of 'themes' or 'stories' to build around. Here are some ideas to inspire you.

TRADITIONAL

ROMANTIC

ETHNIC

STYLISED

59

Hats are fun and can dramatically alter a fairly ordinary look. Everyday felts and classic trilbys can look wonderful. Keep smarter, more delicate creations for special occasions.

therefore less noticeable. If you want your jewellery to be bolder and to contribute towards a stronger look, you need to investigate costume jewellery. There are lots of young designers who are producing fabulous, inexpensive pieces in a variety of materials and styles. Have a look for their work in craft and design centres or local markets. Buying accessories from a more established costume jewellery designer can be considerably more expensive.

Over the last few seasons, the trend has been for jewellery to be bolder and more extravert and there are now countless styles to choose from. Chunky gold generally adds warmth to your outfit whereas silver has a cooler, more stark feel. Glitzy diamanté and coloured stones add instant glamour for the evening, but use them with discretion. More recently, there has been a strong ethnic influence, with lots of fancy metal, wood and various colours of agate used in designs.

Whatever jewellery you choose, make sure that it accessorises the look which you are creating. Its function is to co-ordinate and complement your style. A few well-chosen pieces will be far more effective than lots of jewellery thrown on together. You can, however, be freer when accessorising ethnic looks which often require several bangles, dramatic necklaces and larger, more intricate earrings.

Scarves

A scarf can alter an outfit more dramatically than most accessories. Its size, print and fabric texture all add an extra, individual element to the outfit as a whole. Scarves range from being extremely cheap and cheerful, to fabulous – and expensive – works of art. Scarves give you the opportunity to use colour to its full advantage and to contrast or tone with your outfit.

Take note of how and where scarves are being worn. You can always capture the mood of current styling by precise use of accessories.

TYING THE KNOT!

Tights

When deciding which tights to wear with a particular outfit, choose the weight of tights according to the thickness of the clothes. Accordingly, a thick wool dress looks better with thick or even woolly tights. Similarly, a sheer, silky outfit will be complemented by fine, glossy tights. Colours can be opaque, contrasting or toning, depending upon the look you are creating. 'Fancy' tights are for evenings only.

Sunglasses

Sunglasses can be a very chic accessory and should be chosen to co-ordinate with your total look. Again, it is worth investing in a good quality pair. They will look chic, fit more comfortably and they will last longer. More importantly, a good pair of sunglasses will protect your eyes in strong sunlight, thereby preventing premature crow's-feet and wrinkles caused by screwing up your eyes against the sun.

Sunglasses are NOT the same as ski glasses. They have not been designed for skiing and will not cope with the unique intensity of light or the special weather conditions which you may encounter. The best idea is to buy your ski glasses at the resort. You will usually find a much wider and more chic selection than can be bought at home.

Spex

The prime function of glasses is, of course, to improve your eyesight. Ideally, your spectacles should also slot in easily with your clothes, both for day and for evening. This is a pretty tall order for almost any style

so, if you can afford it, invest in a second pair for a contrasting look. Glasses are expensive, so it is best to avoid extremes and gimmicks which will date quickly. There are a variety of designer frames available which often look fabulous, but remember that they are usually styled to go with high fashion looks and may not fit in with your everyday wear.

As well as complementing your clothes, your glasses should also suit your shape of face. Here are some basic guidelines to help you choose:

Square Face: You have a strongly defined bone structure. Look for rounded or curved frames which will soften the angles of your features. Make sure that the outer corners of the frames span the width of your cheekbones.

Round Face: Avoid round frames and wide lens shapes which will accentuate your round features. Look for rectangular frames which will emphasise the upper and outer corners of your face.

Oval Face: Most types of frames will suit you. If your face is heavier, choose a thin, slightly angular frame. For a thinner face, choose a slightly rounded design which will give an illusion of fullness.

Heart-shaped Face: The emphasis of your face is on the upper half. Spectacles which are rounded or heavier on the bottom work well.

Pear-shaped Face: Try glasses with broad rims to emphasise the upper part of your face.

Scarves can be an effective way of accessorising and adding colour to an outfit and they are useful for when your hair is not up to scratch. Opposite we show simple ways to utilise scarves or fabric. *Left* Simple bow tied in a longer plait. Use a covered elastic band underneath to keep the plait in place. *Middle* Band of fabric fastened on top of head with ends tied in a bow. Make sure the size and position of the bow is flattering to your face shape. *Right* 'Seventies' revival! This requires a fair-sized lightweight fabric. Place scarf on head as if to tie at the nape of the neck. Cross ends and twist into narrow 'string'. Secure with a knot either on top of head, or wind round to nape and secure.

CHAPTER FIVE

Stocking Your Wardrobe

★ Research ★

★ Budgeting ★

★ The sales ★

★ A wardrobe checklist ★

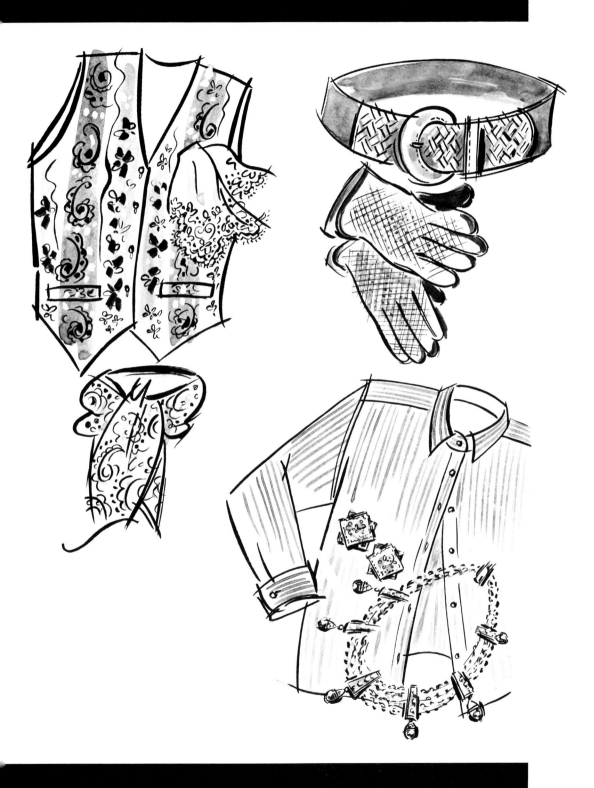

You have taken a long, hard look at your clothes and accessories, as well as your lifestyle. You now know precisely what you want and what you need. It is essential that the new garments which you purchase are functional and work within your clothing scheme.

Research

Before you rush straight out on a shopping spree, it is essential to research fashion and style trends — you do not want to make any expensive mistakes.

The new season's designer collections are shown to the Press and the fashion buyers in March and September every year. All the newspapers, as well as the more upmarket glossy magazines, carry reports from the Paris, Milan, London and New York shows. Make a point of reading the fashion features and take note of the predominant shapes and colours that are being shown.

The expensive end of the market will feature new directions first. Have a good look around high fashion 'designer' shops. Observe the ways in which styles, colours and accessories are used. Do not worry about price at this stage — the idea is not to buy but to give you an idea of current and future style and direction.

The fashions and trends in the designer shows and shops will, before very long be translated into garments which are available in the high street. A lot is lost along the way. Different, less expensive fabrics are used, costly trimming and detailing has to go. The end result is often a very diluted version of the original idea.

By keeping an eye on fashion trends, you will be able to spot good purchases at a glance. Through your knowledge of the more exclusive end of the market, you will immediately be able to translate it into practical use at the less expensive end of the industry. You will be able to spot innovative influences of colour, shape and style the minute they hit the high street.

Fashion foibles

Avoid buying clothes which are too current or faddish. You, and everyone else will tire of them within a few weeks. Beware of sudden, and extreme, swings in colour trends. They do not, as a rule, last and you will end up with garish items which you will not be able to wear more than a few times.

Within every mass market range there are a few unusual, interesting garments which are particularly good value and will have a long 'shelf' life. If you have done your research properly, you will be able to recognise these more enduring items.

Try to make the bulk of your purchases at the beginning of each season, around September or March, when shops are introducing new stock. Some shops stagger their stock and introduce it in phases or themes throughout the season. Find out when this is planned, otherwise, having researched for your new wardrobe, you may still miss out. Another option is to go shopping at the end of the season, during the sales. Look for genuine reductions in good shops. It often pays to buy a garment out of season and to put it aside for a few months — if you have the will power!

Think first

Before you go shopping, have a clear idea in your head of precisely what you want to buy. Make a list of the shops which you are going to visit in order to find the item(s). Armed with a clear shopping strategy, you are far more likely to find what you want, and will also find the expedition less stressful.

DAY INTO NIGHT

DAY SUIT

In order to achieve a chic, daytime style try your 'Chanel' style suit with soft, tie neck blouse or fine roll-neck sweater. Add gold or fancy chains, bracelets and earrings. Coordinate the look with flat pumps and a simple shoulder bag.

EVENING SUIT

For the evening, pare down your accessories. Keep the neckline simple. Wear the suit on its own, or if you prefer, try a silk vest underneath. Jettison extra jewellery – wear stunning earrings and perhaps a bracelet too. A small, feminine shoulder bag and mid-heel court shoes will complete the look. Emphasise lips and eyes when making up. Accentuate your hair style but keep it simple.

Budgeting

The first thing to do when you are contemplating going shopping is to ascertain exactly how much you have to spend. This sounds boring and pedestrian, but it is VITAL. Clothes can involve considerable expense.

Your research will have given you invaluable guidelines. You will have a good idea of maximum and minimum prices for the garments which you are contemplating buying. Ask yourself a few questions: What is the purpose of the garment? How long will you expect it to last? How versatile is it? You will be less likely to wildly overspend on impulse if you give some thought to what you need and how much you can spend BEFORE going shopping.

Economise where you can and spend where you consider that there is no alternative. For example, if you decide to buy a designer jacket in a sale, it may be possible to buy the rest of the outfit inexpensively in the high street.

The heaviest expenditure will be for autumn/winter. Fabrics must be heavier and of a good quality to give you lasting wear. Winter clothes are worn for a much longer period of time than summer wear and must last. You can spend less on summer outfits because they are usually subjected to hard wear for only a few weeks.

Golden shopping rules

Beware of changing rooms. Many are totally inadequate. There is seldom sufficient space and the lighting is usually hopeless. Make sure that you look at the garment in daylight to see what the colour really is. Have a good look at the back view – it is important to get an all-round image.

★

Avoid spontaneous buys. If you see something which you fall madly in love with have a break, a coffee, a moment's reflection. If, after further contemplation, you still want to buy it,

It is easy to create a different look from a basic outfit through altering accessories. Remember – good quality accessories are vitally important; they last far longer, allowing you to accumulate a larger stock of items to play with! Gimmicky bits and bobs are only worth buying if they are cheap.

S
T
O
C
K
I
N
G

Y
O
U
R

W
A
R
D
R
O
B
E

A classic group of basics which will last and last.

Spend as much as you can afford on these items.

'ETHNIC'

This style comes in many different forms. Shop carefully for well-priced pieces which will slot in amongst existing garments to give a fresh look.

'RIDING'

Another lasting look. These items recur again and again.

show it to that faithful friend of yours for a more objective opinion.

Do not keep buying items in the hope that they will slot into your existing wardrobe. This may work with the odd top, but nothing else. Have the confidence to buy clothes which you REALLY want. Go for a total look.

The sales

This section is dedicated to a very close friend of mine who adores exceedingly expensive clothes. When she can afford it, she loves nothing better than blowing a vast amount of money on a fabulous outfit. Come sale time, she indulges in her favourite sport:

1 *THE COUNTDOWN*

She makes a point of knowing the sales assistants in her favourite shops. They advise her of when the sale is scheduled for. During the season, she makes several visits to the shop to try on different outfits and decides what she wants to buy.

2 *THE STRATEGY*

She will be the first through the doors on the opening morning of the sale. Occasionally, she may make an immediate purchase. More often, she carefully monitors precisely what is on offer . . .

3 *MONITORING*

She calls into the shop several times during sale week to ensure that the items that she has earmarked are still there, and to make a note of any further reductions.

4 *SUCCESS*

It is the final day of the sale. My dear friend will have successfully bought items which she has had her eye on for several months, at a fraction of their original price. Her strategy certainly works because she is renowned for obtaining the most fantastic bargains.

Sales hints

Shop in places which you are familiar with. You will know the merchandise and are, therefore, less likely to make a mistake.

If you decide to shop in large central stores or shopping malls, choose labels which you know. You will be able to gauge whether the item is genuinely marked down or not.

Do not buy merchandise which has been specially bought in for the sale — it will not be a bargain.

Check whether goods are faulty.

Resist the temptation to buy anything simply because it is reduced.

Do not feel rushed. Try clothes on as you normally would.

Keep the receipt. You are still entitled to return items if they have been sold as perfect and are found to be damaged.

A wardrobe checklist

This checklist serves as a basic guideline of the garments we require to build up the skeleton of a versatile wardrobe.

Of course, everyone's clothing requirements vary according to lifestyle and spending power, but have a look through the list before you rush out to the shops.

Casual wear/day wear

Two loose, comfortable track-style outfits, in sweat fabric. If you choose bright colours, try to ensure that they are complementary so that you can mix-and-match.

★

A pair of blue jeans – loose styles are usually more comfortable and more flattering. These most versatile of garments are useful in summer and winter, and can be dressed up or down, according to the occasion.

★

Two casual tops. These could be T-shirts, cotton blouses or sweat shirts. A white cotton top always looks great with jeans.

★

A baggy jumper or cardigan for cooler weather.

Formal working environment

Two smart, conventional skirt suits, one in a heavy fabric and the other in a lightweight fabric. Alternatively, try interchangeable skirts and jackets. Choose styles which are not too tight or too short. Longer, hip skimming, blazer-style jackets will prove to be more versatile, should you want to wear them for dressier occasions.

★

Two formal blouses in colours which will complement the suits.

★

A fairly long cotton or cotton-mix dress in a neutral colour, for hot weather. Try to choose a simple style and shade which will look good under one of the suit jackets.

★

A large, long coat – preferably a trench coat – which you can slip over your shoulders when the weather turns colder.

Formal restaurant wear

A fitted, beautifully tailored suit, perhaps in a more extrovert colour than your work clothes. You may be able to dress up one of your work suits for the occasion – use bold, eye-catching jewellery.

★

A soft, silk top to complement the suit.

Party/club wear

The 'little black dress' can be accessorised to meet most occasions. Avoid extreme lengths or a very tight style which may go out of fashion very quickly.

★

A pair of well-cut trousers in a glamorous fabric – silk if you can afford it – are perfect for those occasion when the dress would be too 'dressy'.

★

A fairly loose, well-cut top to complement the trousers, possibly in the same fabric. Avoid a very revealing style which may prove to be unsuitable for more formal occasions.

Holiday/weekend wear

A comfortable cotton dress.

★

A pair of shorts. Baggy shorts are always more versatile and stylish, however young or slim you are.

★

Two short-sleeved/sleeveless T-shirts.

★

A pair of loose, lightweight cotton trousers.

★

A plain cotton sweater for cooler weather.

Accessories are, of course, the key to the success – or failure – of any wardrobe, however basic. Have another look at the advice given on page 56.

CHAPTER SIX

Dressing the Part

★ The business interview ★

★ The two-day business trip ★

★ Socialising ★

★ Holidays ★

★ The wedding ★

There are many occasions in our lives when our normal, everyday style has to be adjusted according to the particular role we are about to play or to our surroundings. For example, attending a high-flying job interview or going on a long, exotic beach holiday, would call for special planning and thought.

You want to look competent, capable, relaxed and stylish, whatever the occasion. The clothes which you wear have a strong influence in determining the way in which you project your personality. You play the role which your clothes have cast you in. Wearing the wrong clothes for the wrong part can be very trying — and embarrassing. Think of the times when you have been caught out!

In this chapter, we take you through some situations and roles which we are all likely to come across at least once in our lives. There will, of course, be countless others. Hopefully, you will be able to adapt the information in this book to deal with them.

The business interview

The clothes which you choose for an interview are usually along the same lines as those which are worn to most offices. Often, people working within accountancy, law, property and many other professions, are still expected to conform in their dress style. Only in 'artistic' fields are people allowed to wear more individual clothes. Dressing for an interview is simply a more calculated and refined version of normal office wear.

You want to be in control as much as possible and to leave nothing to chance. Give yourself plenty of time to style yourself and to work out your interview strategy.

Choose an outfit which is smart, co-ordinated and comfortable. A simple suit, skirt and jacket, or a dress, are safe bets. The clothes should not be too tight — you need to be able to sit down comfortably and to remove your coat and jacket with ease, if you want to. You should not wear anything which is too eye-catching or too exaggerated or over-accessorised. You want to present a professional appearance, so a little jewellery, polished shoes and a co-ordinated look are enough. At this stage, your main task is to make a favourable impression in the ability and personality stakes: you do not want to be remembered solely for your clothes sense! Once you get the job, you can gradually relax into it and introduce looks which are a little more interesting, if you want to. Let the dust settle first!

Grooming is essential. Make sure that your hair is freshly washed and that it looks neat. Clean your face and apply some fresh make-up, but not too much. Make sure that your nails are clean and that you have a spare pair of tights with you. Before you set off, spend a few minutes going through some deep-breathing and stretching exercises for relaxation.

The two-day business trip

Women have now made their mark in most business fields. Consequently, many women are having to travel more frequently. Dressing for the short business trip can be tricky because you do not want to take a lot of luggage, but there are strong pressures on you to look smart and slick and to ring the changes.

Wear a skirt suit for the journey. Pack an extra shirt or blouse, some alternative jewellery, a coloured silk or chiffon scarf and a different pair of shoes. The extra items can be used on the second day to create a different look. Accentuate the new image with different make-up and a slightly altered hairstyle.

If you know that you will have to

attend a fairly smart dinner in the evening, pack an easy, fairly uncrushable dress which will work well with your accessories. Ask the hotel laundry to tidy up your clothes – get your blouse ironed and your suit pressed ready for travelling back the next day.

Obviously you will also need something to sleep in, changes of underwear and extra tights. Your clothes, accessories and toiletries should be packed into a lightweight, small travel bag.

Socialising

There are lots of occasions when socialising requires more formal dress. For instance, smarter dinner parties, dinner dances and balls all demand that a special effort is made. Invitations are usually received well in advance, giving you plenty of time to plan your outfit. Take note of whether the expected style of dress is mentioned on the invitation. If not, ask your host or, if it is a larger formal occasion such as a film première, contact the organisers. Don't be embarrassed – asking beforehand is infinitely preferable to turning up in unsuitable clothes.

The first thing to consider is that this type of outing can knock a large hole in your bank account. Work out your budget. If you have seen a dress you like, find out how much it costs. Decide whether you will need new shoes, evening bag or jewellery. Will you want to get your hair or nails professionally seen to for the occasion? If it all seems prohibitively expensive, why not hire a dress? It will leave you with more money to spend on the extras. There are lots of excellent dress-hire shops which stock a good selection of traditional, period and current designer dresses.

Decide what you are going to wear well in advance, and stick to it. If you are planning to buy the outfit or accessories, do so as early as possible. Try everything on together making sure that the shoes, bag and jewellery look good with the dress. Never buy or hire anything which is not absolutely comfortable. You have to be able to move easily and with confidence. There is nothing worse than feeling awkward or over-aware of your clothes – it will ruin the occasion.

Although you are dressing up, do it subtly. It can be very tempting to go totally over the top with very high heels, fancy tights, lots of glitzy jewellery, dramatic make-up and a complicated hairstyle! Very few events warrant it. If possible, talk to friends to get a feel of the event. You can then gauge how far you should go. You want to look fabulous and stylish, not like a painted doll!

Holidays

On a stress rating level, holidays can feature very near the top. Even if you have chosen the most organised holiday in the world, you will have lots of different situations thrust upon you which you have got to cope with. Many

---

Before you go

If you are travelling further afield, find out about inoculations well in advance.

★

Make sure that your passport is valid. If it is the first time that you are travelling with your child (children) remember to add them to your passport.

★

Apply for any visas which you may need.

★

Apart from traveller's cheques, take a little local currency with you.

★

Pack a few basic medical items such as plasters, a sunburn ointment and a remedy for upset stomachs.

Remember to slot a kanga, sarong or simply a length of fabric into your holiday suitcase. It will prove the most versatile item you could wish for on the beach.

1 *Sundress.* Hold around body from back to front and knot at bust level. Make sure that you have ample overlap and that knot is firm. If necessary use a nappy pin underneath to secure.

2 *Twist-top.* Use a piece of fabric which is large enough (a) to knot at back of neck and (b) to twist at bust level and tuck ends round back to secure with small knot.

Tie-skirt. Make sure fabric is large enough to overlap.

3 *Wrap-top.* Place around shoulders like shawl and knot ends in middle of back to give cap sleeve effect.

Front-flap shirt. Allow sufficient fabric to give ample flap.

people find holidays hard going. Family breaks, the time when everyone is longing to be together, can turn into a nightmare, leaving you crawling home utterly exhausted and dying for a REAL holiday. The kids have had a great time. Mum and Dad are totally wiped out!

What we will do in this section is give you a rough outline of what you will need to take with you on a selection of basic types of holiday. Remember, wherever you are off to, take the MINIMUM you think you will need. You are not moving house and someone will have to carry your suitcase. If it is you and it is heavy, you will regret it. If it is someone else, you will not be very popular and they will regret it even more!

Trip A
Our first trip takes you and your man via the cheapest charter flight that you could find to Corfu and then on to a sun soaked small Greek island by ferry. You are planning to stay in a room which you will rent when you get there. The aim is to keep the cost to a minimum. Discounting flight delays, you will be there for about two weeks, primarily to soak up the sun.

ALL TIED UP!

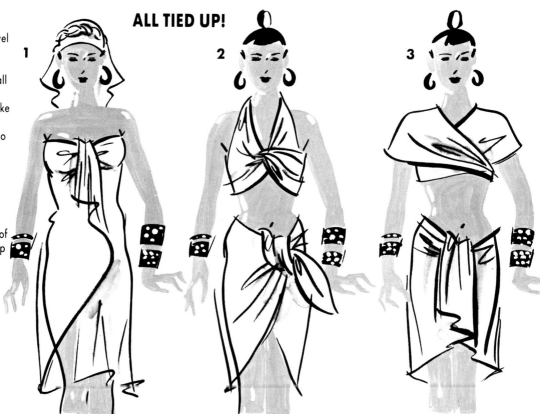

1   2   3

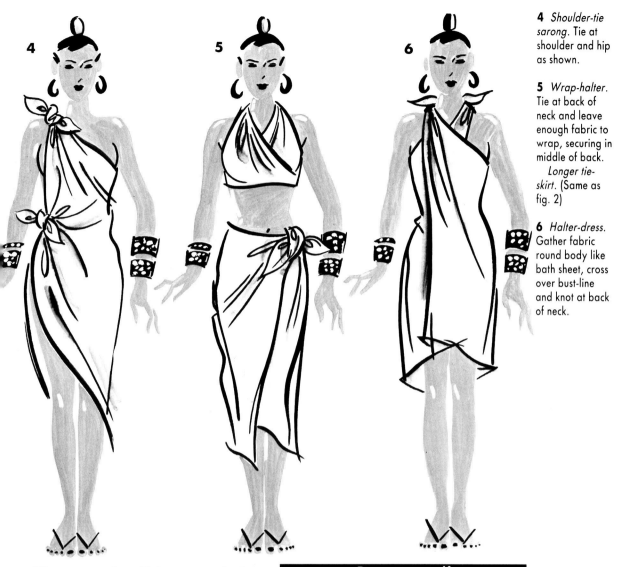

4 *Shoulder-tie sarong.* Tie at shoulder and hip as shown.

5 *Wrap-halter.* Tie at back of neck and leave enough fabric to wrap, securing in middle of back.
Longer tie-skirt. (Same as fig. 2)

6 *Halter-dress.* Gather fabric round body like bath sheet, cross over bust-line and knot at back of neck.

Use a soft, light travel bag, preferably with a long shoulder strap. Make sure that you have easy access to your toilet bag, should you require a quick spruce up on the journey. Try to leave your hands free – it makes life much easier when you are climbing on and off ferries and stumbling into local taxis or buses.

So, what should you pack? Perhaps most important; several pieces of swimwear consisting of bikinis and extra bottoms. A swimsuit on a sun holiday is only of use if it is lightweight and can be rolled down to expose extra flesh. Avoid thick fabrics – they are far too sweaty and uncomfortable and they stay wet for too long. Choose cotton, cotton/lycra or fine lycra. Good quality, more expensive swimwear will keep its shape for longer. You will also need plenty of thin, light and comfortable underwear. Several loose, comfortable

Protect yourself

Take a reputable brand of suncream and aftersun lotion with you, preferably with a high protection factor. There is usually a far better choice of these products here than you will find abroad. Protect your hair on or off the beach with gel or conditioner.

T-shirts are essential. Take a sarong with you – this versatile garment can be used as a hasty cover-up, an extra skirt for the evening or to lie on while sunbathing. Cotton shorts and comfortable sandals or espadrilles are also essential.

Pack a variety of hair accessories to keep your hair off your face. Fine scarves, pieces of fabric, bands, combs or covered elastic will all do. A good quality pair of sunglasses will add some style while protecting your eyes. Pack two evening outfits – they can be shirts, skirts, trousers or dresses. You will be astonished by the additional permutations you will be able to create out of these basics. Add some earrings or bangles; tie your hair back for an evening look. This is where some of your new-found styling expertise comes into play.

You will need an extra pair of sandals or shoes. Do not take delicate, strappy high heels – they will not last a minute on rough stony roads.

There are certain items which it will be well worth buying once you arrive. These include: an inexpensive straw hat to shade you; a cheap local beach mat (infinitely preferable to dank beach towels); cheap plastic sandals for pebbly beaches, a colourful straw bag to put your extras in.

Trip B

You want to see more of Britain and have decided to drive to Scotland, breaking your journey with an overnight stop in the Lake District. Your trip will embrace two or three days at the Edinburgh Festival. It is a ten-day trip and the weather cannot be relied upon. There is no easy solution to this type of holiday. It is mostly down to guess work and a quick prayer.

Pack your clothes in a fairly hard suitcase — it will keep them pressed.

Essential items to be included are a raincoat, walking shoes and a telescopic umbrella. Even if it is very wet, you want to be able to function reasonably comfortably outside. The bulk of your clothes should be practical, comfortable day clothes. Sweat fabric is a good idea — it is soft and comfortable and withstands packing and repacking without creasing. Mix and match your T-shirts, sweatshirts and sweatpants for maximum use. Jeans tend to be a bit stiff and starchy, particularly when you are driving for long distances.

Do not forget your swimsuit. You never know, the sun does shine in the North. Northumberland and Scotland have some beautiful, deserted and unspoilt beaches. You might just feel like jumping out of the car and taking a dip! You may even want to sunbathe.

Take an outfit with you for the evening. It is always useful to be able to pull something fresh and fun out of the bag, should the need arise. What about an easy outfit in flimsy, lightweight silk? Remember your shoes and accessories to go with it.

Trip C

You are off on a three-week trip of a lifetime to Australia, Fiji and Thailand. Pack your things in a reasonably large suitcase and an overnight bag. Take a soft, empty, fold-up case with you. You will

Fabrics

For hot holidays always choose natural fibres — they are far less sweaty! Lightweight cotton is usually the most comfortable. Silk can sometimes prove to be clammy and may show embarrassing dark and damp patches where you have perspired. The main drawback with cotton is that it creases easily. One solution is to pack a travelling iron. Another is to hang any creased clothes in the shower room. The steam will remove most of the creases.

If your holiday takes you somewhere not quite so hot, you can pack a mixture of natural fibres with a proportion of synthetics, which will minimise creasing. If a garment is fairly loose, mixed fabrics usually look quite acceptable.

probably buy quite a few souvenirs on your travels and you want to be able to bring them home with ease.

When planning your holiday wardrobe, follow most of the guidelines laid out for **Trip A**, bearing in mind that the weather may be extremely hot and that you are away for an extra week.

Pack lots of thin, soft cotton separates in vivid colours to mix and match. Include some sarongs.

You will probably be dining out and making trips in the evening, so you will need three or four dressier outfits. Take a selection of accessories with you to ring the changes. Remember to use colour to its full advantage. You will look healthy and tanned and will be able to wear quite vibrant shades. Make the most of it!

Trip D

You are going on a week's skiing trip in the Alps. Pack your things into a soft, lightweight bag. Getting to ski resorts often involves a flight followed by a coach journey. The lighter your bag the more hassle-free your journey will be.

Do not pack lots of heavy, bulky clothing. If you have not already got a ski suit, buy a good-quality outfit from

HOLIDAY WARDROBES FOR SUN AND SNOW

a reputable shop. It is a good idea to look through skiing and fashion magazines before you buy, to see which styles and colours are in vogue.

Take at least two sets of thermal underwear with you – it is soft to wear, keeps you warm and soaks up perspiration. Several pairs of ski socks are also a must. A hat will be necessary if the weather turns cold. Pack a couple of thick headbands too – they are very useful for keeping your ears warm if you do not want to wear a hat. Good quality ski gloves are essential not only for keeping out the cold, but to protect your hands when you fall. You will also need a sturdy pair of après-ski boots for walking around the slushy, icy resort.

For the evening, a pair of casual but smart trousers – perhaps a jodpur style – will be very versatile. Take a couple of fine jumpers and two smart shirts to go with them. Do not forget your leather belt and jewellery to accessorise the outfits. It is a waste of time dragging skirts or dresses to a ski resort, but make sure that you can put together quite a chic look – many resorts are very upmarket, and you do not want to feel too casual.

If you are going to an established resort sun blocks and skiglasses are usually best bought on arrival.

If it is your first trip, and you are not sure whether you will want to ski again, borrow as much of the outfit as possible. However, do not make the same mistake as I did. I borrowed a chic, sparkling white ski suit at the end of the season. The outfit quickly changed from snowy white to camouflage brown as I spent most of the time grovelling in the mud and patches of snow on the nursery slopes!

A family holiday

A family holiday with young children can be very exhausting. Try the following hints and tips to make life easier. They apply to every family with kids, whatever the destination.

1 Plan and organise the family's clothes well in advance. Pack your own things first; it is so easy to slide to the bottom of the list as everyone else's clothes are sorted out.

2 Mix and match when packing for children. If it is hot, children do not need much clothing. On the other hand, you want to avoid doing too much washing on holiday. If possible, stick to shorts and T-shirts.

3 If your children are large enough, get them to carry at least their overnight basics on their backs in individual rucksacks. It can be a nightmare if you arrive at your destination with three children's clothing in one large bag.

4 Before leaving, stock up with any medication which your child normally requires. Remember to take an adequate family medical kit with you. If your children are very young find out where there is a local doctor, clinic or hospital. It could affect your choice of destination.

5 Pack some books, basic games, puzzles and colouring books for the journey. A drawing book or large notebook can be useful.

6 Train your children early on to survive away from home without 'comfort' toys. They really do not need them, and neither do you. You can spend your whole holiday searching for these ragged creatures.

7 If your children are at an age when they can enjoy recording some of the events of the holiday, encourage them to collect memorabilia such as postcards (within reason) and to write some notes or keep a diary. These records are great fun to look back on.

8 If you are going to a hot climate, pack a high factor sun cream or total

block for the children. Keep them out of the sun from midday to three o'clock. If the sun is very strong, cover them with T-shirts. Make sure that everyone drinks plenty of water.

The wedding

Here we are going to concentrate on how you, the bride, can look absolutely wonderful on the big day. As soon as the date is set, work out a rough schedule. Start to allot more time to yourself as your wedding approaches. Slow down. Many of us are so used to rushing around at break-neck speed that we continue like this right up to the last moment.

The dress

Amongst the many items which have to be budgeted for, the wedding dress comes very high on the list. Prepare

Fabulous, feminine, truly the dress of a lifetime. Professional wedding shops will be able to give advice on detail of head-dresses, flowers, etc.

DRESS OF A LIFETIME

TRADITIONAL

It's worth considering a designer who will make a dress specifically to suit you. This will ensure a perfect fit. This type of dress will be fairly expensive, but you could choose a style that can easily be worn afterwards.

yourself for the fact this whole affair will probably go wildly over budget. Traditionally, the cost of the dress is covered by the bride's mother, but whoever pays, it must still be budgeted for. The best point to start from is a rough figure in your head which you feel is acceptable. Remember that you also have to buy a veil and, perhaps, a head-dress.

Our ideas on wedding dresses are becoming more and more flexible. The

formal, traditional white dress is available in an astounding variety of styles and 'period' looks. A friend of mine returned from a tour of wedding shops completely bemused. She had viewed everything from romantic *Gone with the Wind* wedding gowns, to 'Victorian', 'Edwardian' and 'Twenties', right through to 1950s ballerina styles! Make sure that you feel comfortable in the style you choose. Should you decide to play out a

BUDGET

For the bride on a tight budget, it's worth having a look at second hand frocks, or inexpensive floral dresses. A dress like this can look fabulous with a froth of white lace underskirts and topped with a straw hat.

Accessories

Accessories are important. You want to look ultra chic. Your accessories should complement and subtly add to your chosen style. Use a small purse rather than a handbag to carry your lipstick. Decide on your jewellery, tights and shoes well in advance.

fantasy and be Scarlet O'Hara for the day, you must be happy and confident playing that part.

Spend a few days visiting lots of different bridal shops, including the more exclusive ones which will have the newest ideas. Like other areas of fashion, bridal dresses reflect seasonal influences. Try on different types of wedding gowns. Often you will like a certain look and when you try it on, discover that it is not right for you.

The rules of shape, balance and proportion still apply. If you are small, avoid fussy or frilly styles – they will not be flattering. They should also be avoided by larger, rounded women whose size will be accentuated by the extra detailing. Taller, more slender girls can indulge in fancier styles.

If you do not want to wear a white dress on your wedding day, it is possible to buy gowns in a variety of different colours. Choose a shade which is flattering and feminine. If you are getting married in a registry office, there are countless options open to you. What about a beautiful dress or suit which could be worn again afterwards?

Hair

The neckline of your dress dictates, to a large extent, how you will wear your hair. Low necklines are fairly flexible. They look good with longer hair or with tresses piled on top of the head. Short, softer hairstyles will also suit this neckline. High necklines are more tricky. They will look more attractive if the hair is clear of the neck, whatever the length.

Visit your hairdresser and plan your wedding hairstyle as soon as you have decided upon the dress. It is a good idea to take your head-dress and veil with you, so that you can assess your hairstyle accordingly. A word of caution – now is not the time for drastic restyle. You may regret it and feel terrible on your wedding day.

Making the body beautiful

Once the arrangements for your clothing and accessories are under way, you need to start thinking about the body under the dress – from head to toe. You could probably do with some pampering: aromatherapy, a massage, a Turkish bath, a sauna? This above all times is when you should indulge yourself. Tidying, grooming, waxing, trimming, bleaching must all be thought about.

Why don't you spoil yourself? Indulge in two sets of the flimsiest, naughtiest, sexiest underwear you can imagine. Go for it – stockings, suspenders, the lot! One set is to be worn under your bridal outfit, the other for the honeymoon. HE will love it, YOU will love it!

If you can afford it, find out which of these services you can have in the comfort of your own home. It can be extremely beneficial, saving you travelling time and frayed nerves.

Good grooming!

For the most important day in your life you, the groom, should also look and feel good. Allocate some time for preparation. Pamper yourself; diet; exercise; get fit. Remember to organise important details such as a haircut and a professional shave. You could even treat yourself to a manicure. Whatever outfit you choose, it should not only look good, but feel comfortable. If you are having a formal wedding, choose a best man who can organise a lot of these details for you. You want to enjoy the day without being bogged down with trivia.

The bride is important – you are, too!

Wedding tips

Department stores focus on the 'bridal season' from February until the end of spring. They feature beauty workshops, fashion shows and so on. Have a look for ideas, but do not forget that it is a selling exercise.

*

Bridal hire is wonderful way of having the dress of your dreams for the day without breaking the bank.

*

Insurance can be bought to cover such disasters as loss of the bridal gown or cancellation due to illness.

Wedding guests

Having given the bride and groom some thought, it is important not to overlook bridesmaids, pageboys, family and friends, and last, but by no means least, another vitally important person who will want to look especially good on the day – Mother!

Whether you are playing a key role at the wedding, or a less important part, it is essential that you look good, without forgetting the golden rule – budget. If you are buying an outfit specially for the wedding and your budget is limited, shop around for an outfit with simple, well-cut lines, which you will be able to accessorise and wear to a variety of occasions afterwards.

Bridesmaids and pageboys

It is essential that the garments chosen for the attendants will complement the bride and groom. The group should be thought of as a whole, because this is how they will be seen, and how they will appear in wedding photographs. Your weding snaps will be around for many years, so avoid choosing gimmicky styles. Make sure that the clothes are comfortable and made in a fabric which can be cleaned. For younger children, the excitement and demands of the day will be fairly exhausting, so it is not fair to put them into uncomfortable, itchy, tight clothing.

If possible, choose outfits for the bridesmaids and pageboys which can be worn after the event. For girls, it should be possible to find a dress which can be adapted for parties. For boys, shorts and shirts can be used again for smart occasions. Have a good look around at what is available within your price range, then cost the extras.

Remember that a visit to the hairdresser to accommodate bands, headdresses and flowers may be necessary for children, as well as for adults. Make sure that you book the appointments well before the wedding.

Mothers

Choose a simple, chic outfit which you feel elegant in, and which is comfortable and easy to wear. Take note of what the other members of your group will be wearing, and avoid colours which would be too loud or would clash. Hats are fabulous, but if you are unaccustomed to wearing anything on your head, choose a style which you can put on and then forget about, not a fabulous creation which you are constantly conscious of as it slips over one eye! Choose comfortable shoes and plan your accessories – gloves, shoes, purse and lipstick – to co-ordinate. Your purse should be small, carrying only necessities such as lipstick, tissues and powder.

Fathers

Hiring a suit for the wedding is usually a sensible option for most proud fathers. Visit a large, reputable firm well in advance of the wedding and ask their advice about what is in vogue, and what would be suitable for the event. Choose a suit which is comfortable and unrestrictive – it is vital that you feel relaxed on this important day. Treat yourself to a haircut, a manicure and a professional shave on the morning of the wedding.

Friends and relatives

Even if you are only a distant relative or casual acquaintance of the bride or groom, it is still important to wear a smart, attractive outfit to the wedding. Remember, however, that it is the bride's special day, so don't attempt to outshine her by sporting a voluptuous, see-through 'designer' dress, or anything which will draw the attention away from the bride. White, too, should never be worn by anyone except the bride.

CHAPTER SEVEN

Style Stages

★ Pregnancy ★ Baby dressing ★

★ Kid's style ★

★ Teenagers ★

★ The twenties ★ The thirties ★

★ The forties ★

★ The fifties and sixties ★

★ The seventies and eighties ★

ROOM FOR EXPANSION

For Day: For maximum comfort choose sweatshirt and stretch fabric garments. Remember to look for elastic waists. Wear comfortable flat trainers or shoes.

Don't forget to 'style' yourself, by adding interesting accessories. It's just as important at this time to make that special effort.

I f we stand back and take a broad look at our lives, we will see definite phases of development in our dress and our style. In our teens we are experimenting and trying things out; in our twenties we are adventurous and look fabulous in anything; by the time we hit our thirties we know what really suits us, although children and mortgages may make those looks difficult to afford; the forties are the first decade of maturity when confidence flourishes; in our fifties and sixties life becomes less pressurised and our approach to clothes reflects our increased leisure time; in our seventies and eighties the classics come into their own and we can wear them to their best effect.

There are, of course, certain ranges and styles of clothes which look best on a specific age group, but women no longer have to 'dress their age'. We can choose our clothes according to our lifestyles, what we feel confident in and what we *want* to wear.

In this section, we look at basic style stages — not to dictate rules and regulations, but to offer advice and suggestions to help you enjoy dressing for each phase of your life.

Pregnancy

Pregnancy is a very special style stage within many women's lives and it demands a unique approach to fashion and dress. Pregnancy is most

Exercise

Exercise is important throughout your pregnancy, as well as afterwards. Bear in mind how much exercise you are used to. If you normally do very little, take it slowly. If you are energetic and fit, there is no reason to slow down too much. Swimming, walking and well-supervised keep-fit classes are all good forms of exercise. Your doctor will advise you if you are in any doubt.

definitely in vogue at the moment. It has become fashionable to talk about it and to be seen to be pregnant. We can read about how famous mothers cope with the birth and how they feel afterwards; how they manage to incorporate their latest offspring into their already hectic life. It can be very reassuring to share other mother's emotions and problems.

The media's positive approach towards pregnancy has resulted in a generally more enlightened approach towards pregnant women. There is now a much wider range of maternity clothes available and it has never been easier for pregnant women to look glamorous and stylish.

Body heat

As you gradually gain weight, your body will generate more and more heat. Do not buy too many heavy, warm clothes, even in winter.

Comfortable clothes and shoes are crucial during this period. However, your body is going through so many changes that clothes may be the last area that you feel like considering. Friends and family remark on your new relaxed radiance, while deep down, you feel like Humpty Dumpty – normal clothes just won't stretch around where your waist used to be. If you are feeling slightly under the weather, ask a friend to help you to organise your 'look' for the next few months.

The first, and most essential, item to consider is a well-fitting bra. As the months go by and your breasts get bigger, you will probably have to replace it more than once. Go to a shop with a large selection of underwear as well as a professional fitter who will be able to tell you what size of bra you need. Make sure that the straps do not rub or irritate your skin and that it is absolutely comfortable.

Huge sweatshirts, shirts, T-shirts,

For Evening: It's time to dress up. Look your most feminine in a fabulous dress. It's well worth looking through regular ranges which 'happen' to accommodate your expanding waistline. Take extra care with

your hair and make up. Once again 'style' with accessories. Fancy flat pumps can look great with this type of look.

Opposite:
Even the tiniest children look great in an outsize sweatshirt or tee shirt teamed with thicker coloured tights. It's a look which will last and last. There is value for money in buying dungarees a couple of sizes larger than required. You can roll them up, then roll them down! Little girls' dresses can become big girls' dresses if you shop wisely. Choose larger and longer sizes, which look wonderful on little girls, and will look equally good as your little girl gets bigger, but do note this works best with thinner, more flimsy fabrics.

S
T
Y
L
E

S
T
A
G
E
S

90

oversize sweaters and enormous dungarees are ideal for daywear. Clothes should be loose-fitting, attractive and fun. You will also need at least two pairs of well-fitting, flat shoes. If you can, buy a couple of fabulous dresses or outfits for the evening. It is lovely to be able to slip into an extra-glamorous look which makes you feel ultra feminine.

Chain stores stock a good, wide selection of maternity clothes while chic 'maternity' boutiques offer the most tempting collections – at a price! There are also several mail order companies which provide clothes for pregnant mothers. Have a look at regular clothes ranges too. There may well be something amongst them which would fit you. Look for big trousers and skirts with elasticated waists. During the first few months of pregnancy, track pants and leggings with elasticated waists can be worn.

If it is winter, you will need a huge coat or jacket to accommodate the bump. Should you have problems finding one, have a look at the men's ranges, especially in more stylish shops where coats are not so dull and traditional.

Do not spend more than you have to on maternity clothes. Experience has taught me that by the time you have given birth you are so sick of the clothes that you never want to see them again. As soon as you have the semblance of a waist, you will want to wear the sexiest, most outrageous garments possible!

After the event

You have given birth to a beautiful baby. Ecstasy will slowly give way to waves of panic when you scrutinise your body. Although you will have lost a certain amount of weight, it takes about six months for your body to get back to normal, so don't throw those maternity clothes out just yet! Breast-feeding mothers usually lose weight more quickly than those who bottle feed. You must be patient. Post-natal exercises are vital for getting back into shape. Combine a daily home exercise programme with swimming and walking, gradually building up to the same fitness level, if not higher, as before your pregnancy.

When you have given birth to your baby, you still need easy, comfortable clothes which will fit in with your very new role. While your baby is little, right up until the time that he is a large toddler, the clothes which you will be wearing each day need to be hard-wearing. With a spot of clever buying, you can select clothes which will last for a good length of time. Buy lots of separates to mix and match – moderately loose track pants and sweat tops or T-shirts are ideal. Avoid tight clothes. They will not look good while you are still carrying extra weight and, for your own comfort, you want to be able to move around easily.

If you are breast-feeding, your body will retain heat, so wear layers of natural fabrics which you can easily remove if you feel too hot.

If you can resist the temptation, avoid major purchases of clothing — suits and more formal, fitted outfits — until you are back to your normal shape.

Baby dressing

For your baby, choose clothes which are a couple of sizes too big. The sleeves and legs can be rolled up and then extended as the baby grows. Warmth and practicality are vital. Choose soft, natural fibres which are

machine washable. You should even be able to put coats and heavier garments into the machine because, at the end of the day, the chances are that everything will be thrown into the tub.

You need lots of mix and match items for the baby, with elasticated waists. Everything should be easy to

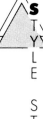
KIDS' LOOKS

take on and off. There is nothing worse than wrestling with a grizzled child, trying to remove clothes which are too tight around the arms or waist, or coping with complicated fastenings.

As your child becomes more mobile, he will retain more body heat and you will find that you do not have to dress him in so many layers. Purchase the toughest dungarees you can find. Even if you have wall-to-wall carpet, crawling will shred the knees of any trousers, however hard-wearing. Holes can be covered with colourful patches.

Correctly fitted shoes are important for little feet with pliable bones. Never economise on your child's footwear. Let him run around with bare feet as often as possible.

Tiny teeth

Good teeth are vital, both from a cosmetic and a health point of view. Your child's teeth are already formed in the jawbone at birth. Look after them by not giving your child sugary drinks and juices.

Milk teeth appear between three months and two and a half years. As soon as the first tooth breaks through the gum, use a soft, tiny toothbrush and fluoride toothpaste, to help strengthen the enamel against decay. Never give juices in a bottle or cup as a comforter to your child − it simply means that his gums and any milk teeth will be coated in sugar for long periods of time.

Kid's style

Children are very aware of fashion and style, and even exceedingly young children can have very definite ideas about how they want to look. This can put tremendous pressure on parents who, while wanting to please their children, cannot always afford to pander to their likes and dislikes. It is essential to begin in the way that you

intend to carry on. *You* must decide how prominently you want fashion to feature in your children's lives and accept the consequences of your decision.

Versatile styles

If you buy your children's clothes carefully, they can last a long time. An elasticated skirt which looks lovely as a calf-length style, can look equally good when your little girl has grown taller and it reaches her knees.

Try to shop without the children for as long as you can get away with it. You will be looking for good quality and good value. If you have young children in tow, you need to keep calm. Do not be rushed into buying something because you have a screaming child with you who wants to go home. If you do make a mistake, most shops will return your money as long as you produce the receipt.

Party time

If you do not want to spend lots of money on party dresses for your little girl, try revamping one which is already in the wardrobe. White or pastel shades can be dyed a stronger colour. Add a length of ribbon around the waist to make it look more exciting. Complement the ribbon with matching hair accessories. It is very similar to styling for grown-ups.

Disregard sizing systems. Your child is quite likely to be above or below average height or weight for his age. Most mothers can see whether a garment will fit their child just by looking at it.

Teenagers

The excitement of becoming a teenager soon settles into the daily demands of surviving and enjoying

DEALING WITH DENIM!

Alternatively, denim and chambray are easy-wearing, youthful classics. Teamed with rich tan-brown leather, the look is chic Western!

Denim is easy to adapt and personalise. Have a go at customising your denims. Simply add a spot of fringing, some buttons, studs, embroidery, or any other idea which takes your fancy.

When you hit puberty, it is as if your whole system goes into overdrive. Large doses of hormones are released into your body so that, as well as the obvious physical changes happening to your body, you feel far more vulnerable emotionally. It is a time when teenagers can need a lot of help and reassurance, but it is not that bad. We have all been through it. It is a part of life and should be tackled as positively as possible.

this period. You are changing very quickly, both inwardly and on the outside. In many ways, it is a transitional phase for you and those nearest you. It is a wonderful time for trying things out and you will have lots of opportunities to develop your ideas about taste and style.

This is the beginning of one of the best periods of your life as regards expanding your interest in clothes. Try out lots of looks and decide which of them suit you. Socially, you will find that you have more opportunities to dress up for special occasions, and it will become increasingly important for you to have a fun wardrobe as well as clothes for everyday wear. You can now begin to create the backbone of a wardrobe which you can easily mix and match. You will also want to collect a few items which are more special and unusual.

There is no point in buying lots of classic garments at this stage in your life. You want hard-wearing everyday clothes with a sprinkling of fun garments to dress up in. Denim slots in perfectly as a youthful 'classic'. Styles alter very quickly, so avoid buying gimmicks or texturing which will date too soon. Jeans and denim or chambray shirts are always handy and easy to style in different ways. You can wear them as CLASSICS, FEMININE, COWBOY or STREET styles. Denim is easy to adapt, whatever new 'looks' hit the headlines.

Style on the cheap

Lack of money is a problem for most teenagers. You want to look good and you have got lots of ideas, but very little money to put them into practice. You need to look at sources of inexpensive but exciting clothing. Most towns and cities have street markets which usually sell reasonably priced clothing. Many young designers who cannot afford to run a shop take a stall at a local market where the overheads are lower and they can sell their garments cheaply. These designers often go on to bigger and better things, so it is fun spotting them at this stage.

Jumble sales can be tremendous fun as well as providing some fabulous bargains. You will, occasionally, find wonderful period garments. Another good source of clothing is second-hand shops. They often stock good-quality, original styles for a fraction of the cost of any similar garment new.

Accessories, even shoes, are often available from the above sources. Start collecting belts, shoes and bags in basic tans, browns and black as well as scarves and jewellery, to style your clothes in different ways.

Even at this level, it is worth looking for reasonable quality. The dress which you bought for £10 and wore just once before it fell apart, turns out to be very expensive indeed.

You will be sweating more, so pay attention tp hygiene. Have a thorough wash every day. Cleanse your skin with unperfumed soap and wash your hair at least twice a week, using a mild shampoo. Avoid any highly-perfumed products which might irritate your skin.

D.I.Y. sewing techniques

Listed below are some easy hints designed for people who can barely wield a needle and thread. Use your

S
T
Y
L
E

S
T
A
G
E
S

TAKE ONE TEE SHIRT

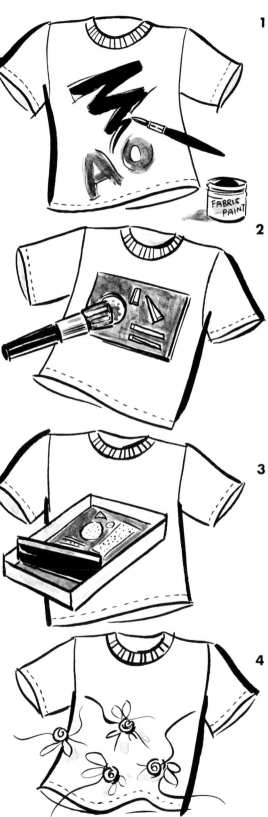

imagination, and give your clothes a new lease of life.

T-Shirts: Cut them into vests for the summer, following the outline of an existing vest. Very loose vests can be worn over a contrasting T-shirt or sweatshirt. White T-shirts can be decorated in a number of simple ways (see illustration).

Leggings: Cut them into knee-length shorts once they are past their best.

Denim Jackets: Add some details with buttons, badges, beads or studs. Apart from the studs, these items can always be removed again.

Jeans: Bleach them, rip them, patch them with contrasting fabric. If all else fails, cut them into knee-length shorts.

The twenties

Your youthful looks allow you to wear anything, as long as you do it with confidence. It is the time when you can try lots of different looks and wear what you want, how you want, so make the most of it. You can even get away with cheap gimmicks and clutter and still look great.

You may not have lots of money, but this should not prevent you from looking stylish. You have to work a little harder to create looks on the cheap. Try buying from inexpensive designers who are still establishing themselves. You want to begin to think about building up the backbone of a classic wardrobe interspersed with fun, frivolous garments and accessories.

Although you think that it will NEVER happen to you, your skin and your body will, very gradually, begin to show signs of ageing. Preventative measures taken in your twenties will pay enormous dividends in later life.

Take one plain T-shirt and express yourself!

1 Paint it. Let your creative spirit run riot. Fabric paints with clear instructions are readily available from most sizeable department stores.

2 Stencil it. Use fabric paint.

3 Print it. Get a book on simple silk-screening techniques from your local library.

4 Tie-die it. Using a basic, cheap, white T-shirt, dye it the colour of your choice 'tieing' a few sections with fine string.

Regular exercise is essential. As well as keeping your body strong and supple, it will ensure that that youthful spring in your step stays with you for many years. There is nothing more ageing than bad posture and a slow, shuffling gait. Try ballet or yoga to keep your body fully stretched.

Avoid spending too much time in the sun, eat sensibly and moderate your intake of alcohol. Boring though these guidelines may be, in years to come you will be glad that you looked after your health and your looks.

The thirties

For the majority of women, spending on yourself is slowing down. Houses and kids are costly and Mum is not quite the priority that she used to be! There are ever-increasing demands that money must be spent elsewhere and you can find yourself struggling to look good on a shoestring budget. Remember that you, as well as the children, need the occasional new garment, so don't sacrifice everything for the family and the home. It is very easy to become a martyr.

Those of you who have remained single have probably elected to take on large financial commitments and have less money to spend on clothes. However, the increased awareness of yourself which age and experience bring, will compensate for having less money and, with a little thought, you will still be able to look good on a small budget.

Whatever the other demands on your time may be, take extra good care of your skin, hair, nails and general health. Good grooming and a healthy skin are never out of fashion.

The forties

No longer is a woman cast on the scrap heap at the approach of her fortieth birthday. This lady is now centre stage; she is the new star. You arrive in your forties a mature, positive woman, with or without children, partners or money to spend on yourself. It is the style stage where confidence flourishes.

There are lots of looks which are fabulous on women of this age. One of the best examples is tailored clothing. Elegant suits look wonderful on this lady; she also looks great in more formal dresses. She will probably reject trousers in favour of skirts, and is looking softer, more feminine.

Be aware of what is going on around you. Observe fashion in the streets, in magazines and in the media generally. Even if it fills you with horror, at least you know what you DON'T want!

One of the trickiest aspects of growing older is assessing when it is time for a change. Nothing looks more dated and unattractive than if you are still sporting dramatically plucked eyebrows from the Sixties, outlined Seventies lips and tatty, shaggy hair combined with a half-hearted attempt at current clothes!

Kids can be incredibly important in offering ruthless honesty. 'Mummy,

The media

There is still very little help and advice on style for the older woman. Television is beginning to turn its attention in this direction, and one or two magazines catering for the older woman have been launched but, so far, progress is slow. From your mid to late forties onwards, you have to use your initiative when you look at fashion magazines. The clothes are often stylish and attractive and you want to rush out and buy them. The drawback is that they are, generally, worn by models who are under twenty. This presents a confusing image for the older woman who finds it difficult to have any idea of whether the style would look good on her or not. If you like the clothes, the only solution is to get out there and try them on!

STYLE STAGES

you're not going to wear that?' is a familiar plea from my daughter who manages to keep me on the straight and narrow. 'Don't you think that skirt is a bit too short?' Staid she may be at the tender age of eight, but her opinion is invaluable. She would rather die a thousand deaths than see her mother the laughing stock of the school playground!

The chances are that a child's view is more objective than that of a doting partner or spouse (if you have one, doting or otherwise). He may have been around you for rather a long time by now, and sees you in a blur, either because he needs glasses or because his image of you is steeped in romantic memories. If the latter is the case, red lights should be flashing – this man needs to bring himself up to date!

The fifties and sixties

There are more people over fifty than ever before. The fall in the birth rate during the Seventies has led to a dearth of youth, while the older decades are flourishing.

Although you may have given up work, life may still be very hectic, especially if you have taken over the care of grandchildren to help working parents. The emphasis of your wardrobe should be on style and comfort. You need attractive, versatile clothes which you can wear without being aware of them. You have been shopping for many years now and your past experience will

enable you to choose comfortable clothes which are also good value.

There are many utterly fabulous looking women in their fifties and much older. I know one exceedingly well-dressed grandma in her mid sixties, who has never looked better. A lady of ample proportions, she is an expert at spotting 'style', co-ordinating it and wearing it. She plans her wardrobe with great care and shops seasonally (every six months). There is never any excuse to let things slide as you get older. It is very easy to look chic, elegant and stylish, so don't let the side down.

The seventies and eighties

A woman in her seventies and older, looks fabulous in classical, stylish clothing. The simple lines of suits, blazers, skirts, jackets and blouses are flattering and easy to wear. Choose base colours which are fairly light and less severe, and team them with attractive toning shirts or fine sweaters. Tweeds can also look fabulous. Avoid fabrics which are too heavy or bulky.

Co-ordinate your clothes with classic, good-quality bags, shoes, belts, gloves and jewellery. An older woman can wear these items to their best advantage.

As for women of all ages, one of the most essential things is to devote a little time to yourself. Spend some time planning and reorganising your wardrobe. Make sure that you take regular exercise and that you set aside part of each day for pampering and grooming yourself.

LADIES' LOOKS

Mature and older women can look wonderfully stylish. Choose softer looks with fluid lines, a style which younger women often find hard to wear. Remember the importance of coordinating your look. Soften hard edges with a scarf. Choose necklines with a tie or some other detail to flatter. Do not forget the importance of accessorising with good jewellery, belts, bags and shoes. Keep your hair well groomed.

Accessories

Train your eye to search out a good buy. You want your accessories to be useful for a significant period, so spend as much as you can afford. Look for co-ordination – never buy one item in isolation. You are not in your teens any more when you could get away with an armful of gaudy plastic bangles, so go for quality and style.

Mature style

With age, a woman's shape softens and matures and her skin and hair alter. These factors have to be taken into account when you buy clothes. The following list pinpoints style features which should be looked for or avoided to achieve a flattering outline.

Necklines: Choose fluid lines in silky fabrics. Avoid hard chiselled revers and stark crew necks, both of which are too severe. Scarves can soften and flatter necklines and jewellery will add interest.

Shoulders: Rounded, feminine lines are always flattering. Set-in sleeves usually provide easier balance. Raglan sleeves are not always successful on an outer garment.

Shoes: Look for a stylish shape which will co-ordinate with your hand-bag. Avoid very high heels and steer clear of fussy, gimmicky detailing.

Skirts: Shorter skirts can look good if you are slim, but don't go too short. Avoid very long skirts – they often look too youthful. Moderation, as always, is the key.

Sleeves: Generally, long sleeves are more flattering than short ones, unless you are terribly fit and brown. Avoid fussy, complicated lines, frills and detailing.

Trousers: Choose classic, simple shapes. Avoid skin tight styles.

Mature make-up

Once you reach forty, it is important to reassess your approach to make-up. Until now, you have probably selected fashion colours and techniques, which may not always have flattered your looks. You now need to emphasise a fresh, healthy look, rather than slavishly following fashion. You should aim to apply lighter, softer make-up, with a more delicate touch. Emphasise your now more transluscent skin by using very little foundation cream, and hardly any powder. It is particularly important to avoid using powder around the eyes, where it will emphasise any wrinkles. Avoid metallic and iridescent eye colours which will draw attention to every small line. Bright eye colours will look too gaudy. Add warmth to your lips by using stronger beige and brown-toned pinks, rose, coral, burgundy or plum. Pale lipsticks are too insipid, and orange and orange-toned and blue-toned reds are too strong. The same advice which applies to your clothes, also applies to your make-up: avoid harsh, exaggerated lines and bright or intense colours, which are too ageing.

If you find it difficult to choose make-up and to apply it, ask for some advice from an expert. A hairdresser or make-up consultant will be only too pleased to help. Remember, do take that faithful friend with you, who has accompanied you on your shopping expeditions – he or she will enable you to be more objective.

CHAPTER EIGHT

It's a Man's World

★ Planning your wardrobe ★

★ Basic styles ★

★ Accessories ★

★ Suit yourself ★

★ Your figure and its faults ★

Many men who head straight for this section will find answers and helpful suggestions relevant to them in other parts of the book. The principle of building a stylish, versatile wardrobe is the same for both men and women. A large proportion of the advice is simple common sense. Often, however, it takes an outsider to offer a fresh slant; an objective view.

Having said this, I feel that it is crucial that men have a separate section. Men are caught in the Eighties/Nineties image machine just as much as women are. It is probably even harder for men to adjust to their new roles, because they have had to evolve so quickly in a short time span.

The mammoth advertising assault on the male market over the last few years and the new slick image of the high street retailer, have caused major earthquakes. Men are more aware of their image and their style than ever before.

Planning your wardrobe

Follow a similar outline to the female wardrobe building plan. Have a good look at what you have and get rid of anything which you have not worn for two years or more. Dispose of all faded, torn or worn garments. At the very least, relegate the offending items to the DIY, gardening or dirty jobs

drawer. If you lay everything which is left out in front of you, you will be able to see precisely what you have and where the gaps are. It will give you a clearer idea of your shopping priorities for the next time you venture out. If you have a doting female in your life, you will know what to ask to be given for your next birthday or Christmas.

You need to plan your wardrobe so that you have basic daywear which is appropriate to your lifestyle, for example suits or overalls, casual clothes for the weekend and garments for socialising and evening wear.

Colour is a good basis on which to organise your clothes. Look carefully at the clothes you already have and decide what your base colours are — black; grey; brown; navy; camel; tan? Team the base colours with complementary colours to tone and contrast. Don't be afraid of bright colours — they can look fabulous, whatever your age. Try black with primary shades; black with neutral colours. Don't be afraid of colour — experiment with new combinations of shades and tones.

Basic styles

Some men naturally take an interest in how they look. For others it is a great struggle, especially now that there is so much choice. Have a look through magazines and style pro-

grammes and decide how you want to look, bearing in mind what you already have in your wardrobe. Choose a style which suits you and which is comfortable and an easy base to build on. The following definitions will assist you.

Italian style

For many men, this look can be a very good starting point. It is current, stylish and understated. It is an easy, wearable classic – a modern-day version of the Mafia sharp-suiting of the Twenties. Remember *The Godfather?* This is it! The look is confident, consisting of high-quality fabrics, loose and comfortable cuts, simple shirts, chic ties, a minimum of accessories and sleek haircuts.

'ITALIAN'

This look can be worn a variety of different ways. The easiest use of the 'Italian' look is as a classic. Simple lines, easy cut, no garish colours. Minimal accessorising. Attention to grooming. Hair in trim. Nails neat. You've got it!

'BUSINESS'

Remember that you need a shopping plan. Do some research first. Look through some magazines, get an idea of what you like, investigate prices and do plenty of window shopping. You are then ready to start making your purchases without the danger of committing yourself to expensive mistakes.

In or out of the office this is a great look. Try to be as creative as possible within the confines of the business suit. It really can look chic. It's all down to the way in which you coordinate shirt, tie, handkerchief, braces, shoes, etc. Remember to balance spots and stripes with stretches of plain fabric.

This style is one of the easiest to wear because it flatters most shapes and heights, including overweight men, because the silhouette tapers gently from the shoulders. Choose jackets and trousers which are loose and comfortable but not quite baggy. The jackets should have padded, rounded shoulders with medium to narrow lapels, no vents and no more than two buttons. The jackets should be long, almost covering the bottom. Trousers should have pleats but not turn-ups.

Remember that this is a look which will last, so it is worth spending as much as you can afford. If possible, buy the garments from a designer sale where quality items can be reduced by up to 50%.

Even if you are on an exceedingly tight budget, a spot of Italian dressing is still possible. Most 'chain' stores have inexpensive versions of this style. For example, start with a simply cut jacket in a neutral base colour (it can have subtle stripes or checks or a slight texture). Grey, navy or subtle non-earth shades of brown, taupe or dull sage would all be perfect. Choose toning sweaters and lighter or neutral shades of shirts or sweaters to complete the Italian look.

Latin style

Recently, Latin style has received a lot of coverage. Think of Spanish dancers in an everyday setting. Sharply tailored jackets, fancy waistcoats worn with shirts with lots of details, even

IT'S A MAN'S WORLD

106

frills, feature strongly. Obviously, this style is for a minority but, as with every strong fashion influence, it will filter through the various levels of fashion and will end up, albeit diluted, on the high street.

College style

A perennial favourite is the all-American college look – with a touch of Ivy League. Originating in the Twenties on campus, it crops up again and again, with only minor variations. To create this look choose loose cotton shirts with button-down collars, three-button sports shirts, Sta-prest trousers and baggy jeans. Complete the look with loafers. A short, smart haircut is essential.

'COLLEGE'

Relaxed, urban-sport look. Not quite fit for the office, but reasonably smart. Essentially a 'youth' style, but can look great on 'Mr. Mature' if you avoid any gimmick and go for a looser fit.

Hair

Don't automatically keep the same haircut as the one you have always sported. It may well be time for a change, particularly if your hair is thinning. A 'crop' looks fabulous on a sparse head of hair – far more attractive than trying to camouflage the bald patch with long strands which lift in the wind! If you have had a moustache for years, why not try shaving it off? If you sport a beard, try some 'designer stubble' or a clean-shaven look. Be brave – experiment. You are never too old to change your style.

Traditional business style

Although stripes are considered to be traditional city clothing, try to avoid the city cliché of a loud pinstripe suit teamed with a bright, boldly striped shirt (with or without plain stiff collar) accompanied by a clashing striped or patterned tie. Each set of stripes and patterns competes with the rest, creating a chaotic, brash image. A pinstriped suit combined with a smart plain shirt and a chic tie are far more tasteful.

The Italian look can be modified to meet the requirements of the most straight-laced office and you will look stylish and expensively dressed.

Currently, men are looking increasingly individual. Clothes are more fun and more flexible than ever. 'Styling' and 'looks' for men are now as varied as for women. It's all a question of choosing your style, then learning to coordinate the look. Buying and using accessories wisely will help you to change the look when you want to.

Accessories

The most important aspect of accessorising your clothes is to ensure that anything which you add helps to co-ordinate the look. Invest in a basic stock of good-quality, neutral accessories.

Belts: A good leather belt will make an inexpensive outfit look more stylish and an expensive outfit superb. Buy the best quality that you can afford – one in black and one in a neutral shade of brown.

Hats: Hats are no longer obligatory in most professions. However, they can add a touch of originality – even eccentricity – to your clothes.

Shoes: Try to accumulate several different shoe styles which will complement your different outfits. For instance, brogues can look superb with jeans and soft, round-toed leather lace-ups look good with baggy trousers. Alternate your shoes, clean them regularly and invest in some shoe trees – your shoes will last much longer.

Socks: Buy good-quality fabrics which will survive frequent washing. Try using socks to accentuate your clothes, for example, wear an Argyll pattern with country-style clothes, or team bright sports socks with trainers and track wear. Textured cotton can look good with sturdy lace-ups and denims. Don't wear outrageously-

Ties

A tie may, or may not be your style. It has been said that a man simply is not dressed without one. In Britain, a tie can still prove to be the single most influential piece of apparel which a man can wear. An old school tie can win or lose you a job. It still rules supreme in the world of finance. Club ties, association ties, military, sports and political ties – one glance and it is immediately clear whether you belong to the right or the wrong group!

coloured socks to an interview or important meeting unless you are very sure of your position. People WILL notice and the chances are that they will not react favourably.

Suit yourself

Suits can be worn lean and straight or loose and more relaxed. If you don't want to blend into the background, try wearing a suit with a 'twist' – a snazzy tie, a bright handkerchief, smart cuff links. What about a flower in your button hole. Try it – in moderation!

If you have an old suit which you really like and cannot replace, choose some fabric, give it to an expert tailor, and have another one made. Bearing in mind the cost of an off-the-peg suit, this can be a viable way of copying your old favourite.

Your figure and its faults

If you are small, you can help to give an impression of extra height by creating fluidity through your clothes. Do not wear separates in sharply contrasting colours – they will cut your height. Instead, aim to co-ordinate colours from head to toe to give the illusion of a few extra inches. Avoid styles which have excess detail such as lots of buttons, fancy seams or fussy pockets. Choose narrow lapels to create an impression of height.

★

Tall men can wear bold and contrasting separates. If you are very tall, you may want to visually loose a few inches by emphasising colours and detailing. Whatever you do, don't slouch.

★

Narrow shoulders can be camouflaged with set-in sleeves and a slightly padded round shape. Avoid raglan sleeves which will emphasise lack of width.

★

Superfluous flesh can be disguised by wearing slightly larger clothes. If in doubt about your sizing, always go one size up. It is far more flattering. Shirts should be larger rather than smaller – buttons straining to meet buttonholes across acres of flesh do not look attractive! Similarly, trousers look ghastly when hooked under a beer gut. Wear a larger size which reaches your waist.

★

Big waists are minimised by avoiding shirts with darts and trousers with fussy pleating. Large bottoms should be covered in loose-fitting trousers. Jackets will flatter your shape if they cover the offending backside.

★

Short legs will be given an illusion of length by wearing trousers without turn-ups and a simple line which fits right up to the waist.

Posture

Whatever your shape and however you choose to dress, it is vital to stand tall. Even the most beautifully cut suit will look terrible on you if you are round-shouldered and your tummy is flopping out. Try to correct your posture for your general well-being. If you find this a problem, try a course of Alexander technique classes which help you to understand and to correct bad habits. General exercise, too, will help.

CHAPTER NINE

Clothes Care

★ A washday manual ★

★ Leather maintenance ★

★ Storing your clothes and accessories ★

★ Spots and stains ★

★ A final note ★

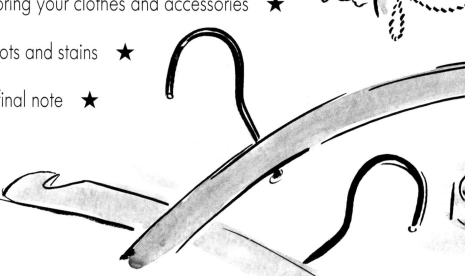

Clothes care can be a bore and a chore — but it definitely pays dividends. A few extra minutes spent on maintenance will help to extend the life of the clothes in your wardrobe. Normally, we tend to take more care of expensive garments, while giving the cheaper items little or no attention. This is rather short-sighted. There is no reason why cheap clothes, given a little bit of care, cannot last just as well as the more expensive ones.

My first hazy memories of caring for clothes go back to the Fifties and an archaic Hoover twintub which my mother wrestled with every Monday. It clanked and clattered, shuddering and reverberating like some huge aircraft struggling to get airborne. If overloaded, it twisted the wet clothes into an enormous rope which had to be manually disentangled — it was like wrestling with a giant serpent! Rinsing was done by hosepipe from the kitchen tap. Spinning was also very primitive with water being removed from the machine by further lengths of hosepipe.

The wash completed, the clothes and sheets were then wrung out manually, folded and solemnly fed through a machined called a 'mangle' which had two hefty rollers through which the wet items were squeezed, and a large handle to wind them through. A tin bath stood underneath to catch the water. The operation was easier with two people in attendance — one to feed the washing through the rollers and catch it at the other side before it hit the floor, and the other to wind the handle of the 'mangle'. Everything was then hung on a rope pulley suspended from the ceiling, which had a nasty habit of breaking under the weight! This was the exhausting ritual which took up most of Monday.

A washday manual

Nowadays, things are a lot easier for most people. However, there are still certain guidelines to follow, even with the most sophisticated washing machine. Learn not to throw everything into it on any old setting. Separate your colours beforehand. Your whites will remain fresh if they are kept well away from any colours however many times you have washed them. Coloured garments will survive longer if you differentiate between pastels and much darker dyes and denims. New coloured items should be washed separately on a lower temperature for the first couple of washes to allow for any dye loss.

Washing
The following guidelines will help you to decide how best to wash items which do not have a label, or that you are unsure about.

Fabrics Dyed With Non Colour-Fast Dyes: Hand-washing is advisable. Use warm water and a mild soap powder, immersing the items for only a few minutes. Wear rubber gloves to protect your hands from the dye.

Fine or Delicate Knits and Pure Wool: Although many washing machines can cope with these fabrics, hand-washing will avoid any disappointments. Squeeze the garments gently in warm water and soap flakes. Do not rub or pull the fabrics.

The stylist's tool box

The following items are essential for a tidy, well-groomed appearance:

★ A two-way clothes brush
★ Cellotape for removing fluff from dark colours
★ Wax and polish for your shoes
★ A suede brush
★ A shoe horn

Most knits can cope with a SLOW spin in the machine to remove excess moisture, but if in doubt, gently squeeze out as much water as possible, ease the garment into shape and dry it flat on a white towel.

Cotten and Linen: If you are washing by hand, use hotter water and a soap powder. White colours should be washed separately from any darker colours. These fabrics can be scrubbed quite vigorously and can, usually, be put in the washing machine.

Drip-dry Cotton: This fabric requires frequent washing, whether by hand or by machine. If you are using a machine, use a short wash setting which will wash and spin the garments very quickly and gently. Avoid scrunching the fabric too much if you are hand-washing it. Hang the garments up to dry when fairly wet.

Synthetics: Wash frequently, either in the machine or by hand. White nylon can cope with hotter temperatures than coloured fabrics. Drip dry to minimise ironing.

Drying

If you live in the country, dry the clothes outside. It gives them an extra sparkle and they will smell wonderful. City dwellers may want to keep their washing indoors! If you have a tumble drier, do not leave the clothes in it for too long – synthetics may shrink and you will probably find that your leggings have become knee-length shorts! You CAN minimise ironing if you have a tumble drier.

Ironing

Most clothes are easier to iron when slightly damp. The result will be a crisper, smarter finish. Heavier cottons and linens should be even damper and then ironed with a hot iron and allowed to air thoroughly. Do

not iron straight onto delicate fabrics – place a thin, clean white cotton cloth between the iron and the garment.

Make sure that you allow all freshly-pressed garments to cool down before you return them to your wardrobe. If you stack them on top of each other whilst still hot, they will end up with lots of creases and you will have to start all over again!

Leather maintenance

Shoe care

Polish your shoes with a neutral shoe cream every day. It leaves an invisble finish on the leather which protects your shoes against scuffs. It also keeps the leather soft and pliable. Use appropriately coloured cream, wax or polish for scuffed boots or shoes.

A very fine rubber sole protects leather soles, preventing the leather from becoming saturated in wet weather. However, make sure that it is put on by a good, experienced cobbler. If your shoes do get soaked, stuff them with newspaper to absorb the moisture and place them somewhere well-ventilated to dry, leaving them on their sides. NEVER dry your shoes near artificial heat – it will destroy the leather.

Handbags and belts

Buff these accessories regularly with a very soft cloth. Occasional 'feeding' with a light non-coloured cream manufactured for the purpose, will keep the leather soft and protected.

Leather gloves

These should be cleaned professionally, although you could try a leather shampoo – follow the instructions carefully.

Spots and stains

If you have a particularly stubborn stain, think before you do anything. Don't panic. Hasty, often wrong, reactions can destroy the garment, leaving the offending spot intact. It is usually impossible for a professional to rectify the damage caused by sloshing on various solutions which have then been scrubbed into the garment. The best idea is usually to take the garment into a good dry-cleaners as soon as possible, telling them precisely what the stain is.

If you do want to have a go yourself, here are some fairly reliable remedies:

Blood: Gently sponge the stain with cold water – hot water will make it permanent. Soak the garment overnight in tepid, soapy water.

Chewing Gum: Place the garment into the freezer and leave it for a few hours. Once frozen, the gum will crack and can be peeled off the fabric. Remove any remnants of gum with white spirit.

Chocolate and Coffee: Soak the garment overnight in a solution of biological washing powder. Wash the garment as normal.

Fruit: Sprinkle the stain liberally with salt to soak up the stain. Wash in warm water.

Grass: Place a clean, absorbent cloth underneath the stain. Soak another piece of cloth with methylated spirit and sponge the stain, taking care not to spread it. Soak the garment overnight in cold water, then wash it in warm, soapy water.

Grease and Oil: Sprinkle with talcum powder to absorb as much of the oil as possible. Alternatively, sponge the stain with liquid detergent. Dilute the detergent for man-made fabrics.

Make-up: Sponge the stain with undiluted liquid detergent. Leave it on the stain for five minutes, then rinse well with cold water. Dilute the detergent for man-made fabrics.

Mild Scorch Marks: These can be minimised by sponging the fabric immediately with a solution of cold water and sugar.

Mud: Scrape off any excess mud, taking care not to force it further into the fabric fibres. Leave the mud until it is completely dry, then brush it using a stiff brush. If the mud has left a stain, sponge the mark with a solution of liquid detergent. Leave the garment to soak in cold water overnight. Wash as normal.

Nail Varnish: Place a clean piece of absorbent fabric or white cotton wool under the stain. Soak another piece of fabric with non-oily, uncoloured nail varnish remover. Gently dab the satin, working inwards, so that you do not spread the varnish. Nail varnish can be very difficult to remove successfully, so if it has been spilled on a treasured garment, you are well-advised to take it to a good dry-cleaner.

Wine: Both red and white wine stains can be removed by sponging a solution of lemon juice and salt over the stain.

CLOTHES CARE

114

When you are cleaning stains, avoid using coloured cloths, sponges or soaps which can transfer colour onto the fabric you are cleaning. Minimise water marks by blotting out excess water with a dry white cloth.

Storing your clothes and accessories

Unless you are very meticulous, the contents of your wardrobe will require tidying and re-organising every so often. Here we will look at the best ways of hanging and storing your garments to keep them looking good.

Invest in padded or rounded and well-shaped hangers. Button, zip or fasten jackets, coats or dresses onto the hanger to keep the garments in shape and to avoid creasing. Buy clip or press hangers for your trousers and hang them full length. Skirts should be hung by the loops – you can easily stitch loops into any garment which does not already have them.

Fold sweatshirts and jumpers with care, so that you do not create any creases. Put the bulky, heavy garments on the bottom of the shelf and pile the lighter ones on top. Hang shirts and blouses if you can. If you do not have enough space, fold them up carefully, without creasing.

Hats should be stored in hat boxes, if possible – cardboard ones are fairly inexpensive. Look for second-hand traditional hat boxes which will protect hats from being knocked out of shape and will also keep soft velours dust-free.

Shoes should be kept in shoe boxes if you have the room. Invest in shoe trees – they will prolong the life of your shoes. Boots, too, should be

Dye it

You may have a garment which you feel is wonderful – apart from the colour. Dyeing is sometimes a solution, but remember that only very pale or white fabrics can be successfully dyed. Darker coloured materials will affect the end result, although they can sometimes be bleached and then overdyed. Make sure that you use the correct product for the fabric that you are colouring, and follow the instructions carefully. If it is an expensive item, or a large, bulky garment, your are well-advised to have it professionally dyed.

protected and fitted with boot trees. They will look like new when you unearth them again at the beginning of the following winter.

The best method for storing tights, socks and sheer socks is to separate the three groups and to keep each of the groups in a separate fabric bag. It will keep them tidy and will protect fine nylons and silks.

Belts will be easier to find if you keep them looped over a hanger. Scarves should be folded in a pile on a shelf where they can easily be seen, and jewellery should be allocated a separate shelf or drawer. If you stack earrings, bangles, necklaces etc. in separate little boxes, it will keep things under control and you can see everything at a glance.

A final note

At the end of the season, dry-clean, wash, repair and store excess clothing to avoid general chaos in the wardrobe. Tuck in some lavender to keep the clothes smelling fresh and to discourage moths.

Index